the grief
recovery
kit

a young person's
guide through the
journey of grief

Aepisaurus Publishing

by Tanya Kilgore

photography by Amanda Marie Harrison
foreword by Terri Savelle Foy

Aepisaurus Publishing
PO Box 5309
Austin, TX 78763
www.aepisaurus.com
© 2011 by Tanya Kilgore

All Scripture quotations, unless otherwise indicated, are taken from the *Holy Bible, New International Version*.® *NIV*.® © 1973, 1978, 1984 by International Bible Society. Used by permission of Zondervan. All rights reserved.

Other Scripture taken from *The Message.* © 1993, 1994, 1995, 1996, 2000, 2001, 2002. Used by permission of NavPress Publishing Group.

Quote from David Kessler used with permission, visit David Kessler at www.grief.com.
Quote from Susan Jeffers, Ph.D. used with permission.
Quote from Agnes de Mille used with permission.
Quote from Steve Goodier used with permission.
Quote from Tim Doyle used with permission.
Quote from E. Joseph Cossman used with permission.
Quote from Paul Dickson used with permission.
Quote from Elisabeth Kübler-Ross used with permission.
Quote from Robert Muller used with permission.
Quote from John Wayne used with permission from John Wayne Enterprises.
Quote from Terri Savelle Foy, used with permission, from *Making Your Dreams Bigger Than Your Memories* by Terri Savelle Foy, published by Regal from Gospel Light, Ventura, California.
Quote from Dr. Seuss used with permission, *One Fish, Two Fish, Red Fish, Blue Fish* by Dr. Seuss, Random House, Inc.
Quote from Zig Ziglar used with permission. For more information from Ziglar, America's Number One Personal and Professional Development Training company, visit www.ziglar.com.
Quote from Max Lucado reprinted by permission. *The Applause of Heaven* by Max Lucado, 1999, Thomas Nelson Inc., Nashville, Tennessee. All rights reserved.
Quote from C.S. Lewis used with permission, *A Grief Observed* by C.S. Lewis © C.S. Lewis Pte. Ltd. 1961.
Quote from Jim Rohn, America's Foremost Business Philosopher, reprinted with permission from Jim Rohn International © 2011. As a world-renowned author and success expert, Jim Rohn touched millions of lives during his 46-year career as a motivational speaker and messenger of positive life change. For more information on Jim and his popular personal achievement resources or to subscribe to the weekly Jim Rohn Newsletter, visit www.JimRohn.com.
Quote from Chuck Swindoll: "Attitudes" is excerpted from the sermon, *Strengthening Your Grip on Attitudes* (SYG7A), by Chuck Swindoll. © 1981 by Charles R. Swindoll, Inc. All rights reserved worldwide. Used by permission. The complete sermon can be heard on-line at www.insight.org.

Principal photography by Amanda Marie Harrison, Amanda Marie Portraits
Cover by Amanda Marie Harrison and Scott Deems
Layout design by Scott Deems, Basement Light Design
Author photo and Resource photo by Carlie Tise
Copy editing by Betsy Friauf

Printed in Canada

Library of Congress Control Number 2011909371

ISBN 978-0-98-35688-0-3

A portion of the proceeds from this book will be donated to organizations that enhance the lives of children needing help and hope.

We would appreciate your feedback and experiences with this book.
Please contact us at contact@aepisaurus.com and share your comments or visit our websites: www.aepisaurus.com and www.griefrecoverykit.com. Additional copies of this book may be purchased at www.griefrecoverykit.com.

Foreword

I have the privilege of speaking to people all over the world about how to overcome the things that keep them trapped in the past and how to accomplish their God-given dreams, goals, and life-assignment. Grief is one of the tools the devil will use to keep people from living their lives to the fullest. The pain of accepting what has happened can be overwhelming and those fighting this battle need more help than simply being told to "move on" with life.

That's why I am so glad Tanya Kilgore has created *The Grief Recovery Kit*. It is a comprehensive resource for children, teens, and adults working through the grief process. Tanya lays out very specific and practical steps to be taken in order to move from brokenness into wholeness. It may not be an easy process, but being proactive in seeking healing will be worth it.

The Bible says that Jesus came to heal the brokenhearted and comfort those who mourn (Isaiah 61:1). My prayer for you as you apply the information in *The Grief Recovery Kit* is that you will experience God's love in a real and powerful way and you will complete down to the last detail what God has assigned you to do (John 17:4 THE MESSAGE).

Terri Savelle Foy
Author, Founder and President of Terri Savelle Foy Ministries

Contents

Introduction

    What is *The Grief Recovery Kit*? 7

    Moving Forward Through Unknown Territory...........9

    From the Author 11

    Dedication 13

ABC's for Parents or Caregivers 14

Stories of Grief and Loss 21

    I Just Want My Daddy Back!...................... 23

    Saying Good-bye 33

    No Tragedies in a Perfect World 39

    Just Gone.. 49

Activities for Your Grief Journey.... 59

Resources......................... 140

My Journal....................... 141

My ~~The~~ Grief Recovery Kit

A Young Person's Guide Through the Journey of Grief

What It Is

This is a healing kit designed to assist young people in the grieving process due to loss, separation, or death. Each person, regardless of age, goes through a grieving process after a significant loss.

When To Use It

When it comes to grieving, there is no way out of it and there is no way around it. With grief, it is best to go straight through it. The loss may include anyone or anything significant to that person. Whatever the case, the painful event should be experienced head-on without avoidance. Trying to ignore the pain or putting off the grief process may cause complications later in life, possibly compounding the grief over time.

How It Helps

Addressing the situation thoroughly and without delay often allows the healing process to start right away. This will help establish a more stable and peaceful heart for the future of the griever. There is no exact time frame for healing, nor is there a precise definition for recovery.

Who It's For

The Grief Recovery Kit was created specifically to help children, preteens, adolescents and young adults come to the reality of their loss and start their own grief and recovery process. However, grievers of all ages can benefit from this resource. This is a tool to aid in the progression of those dealing with the sorrow and pain of their loss as well as provide hope.

What's In It

The kit contains:

* helpful ABC's for parents or caregivers of a grieving child

* four stories of loss illustrated with photography: one from the perspective of a child, one from a preteen, and two from teenagers

* 40 activities that encourage participation of the griever, with a supportive prayer and multiple Scriptures that correlate with each activity

* a Personal Journal for thoughts and feelings in written words or other creative means such as drawings

Moving Forward
Through Unknown Territory

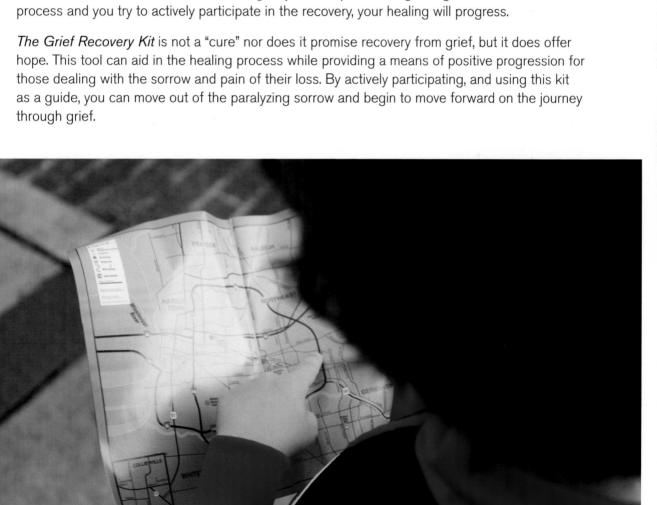

The journey through grief, especially for a young person, can be a confusing and difficult event. There are no specific rules or expectations for the grief journey; there are only suggestions and guidelines.

There is no exact time frame for healing nor is there a precise definition for recovery. Recovery is subjective and can have various meanings to each griever.

The intense pain you may be feeling now will eventually lessen but your fond memories will not. You will always remember and miss your loved one or what you lost, but the pain will ease up.

As a griever, you may wonder how long your grief will last. Everyone is different, as well as their own situation. As long as you are open to the grieving process and you try to actively participate in the recovery, your healing will progress.

The Grief Recovery Kit is not a "cure" nor does it promise recovery from grief, but it does offer hope. This tool can aid in the healing process while providing a means of positive progression for those dealing with the sorrow and pain of their loss. By actively participating, and using this kit as a guide, you can move out of the paralyzing sorrow and begin to move forward on the journey through grief.

From the Author

This grief recovery kit was created to help in the passage of pain, to provide spiritual guidance and to help you move toward self-discovery and hope.

You are not alone on this quest of recovery. With the help of your support system—all the people who care about you—and God, you will progress toward peace and healing.

My prayers are with each of you who carry a grieving heart. I too have experienced sorrow and have been on a journey through grief. These stories were written from my own broken heart after the loss of my dad.

As you progress on your journey, know that you are loved and that your heartache is important to God. This book demonstrates the endless compassion and love that our Heavenly Father has for us, especially in our times of despair.

I pray this message gives hope to the reader for a healing heart, because there is hope for a brighter tomorrow while trusting in the Lord Jesus Christ. I also pray *The Grief Recovery Kit* will touch you in a positive way and help you move toward restoration of the joy and laughter that make our lives beautiful. May God bless you, heal your heart, and be with you every step of the way on your journey through grief… just as He has with me.

Be courageous and boldly go!
Tanya

> "Courage is being scared to death, but saddling up anyway."
> —John Wayne

3 John 1:2 *Dear friend, I pray that you may enjoy good health and that all may go well with you, even as your soul is getting along well.*

The Grief Recovery Kit

Dedication

My daddy was a remarkable man. He was loving, giving, loyal, amusing and extremely funny. He loved his family, friends, strangers and his Lord.

Daddy was a very animated character, which made his nickname so appropriate. Most people never knew him by any other name. He was tall, lofty and hilarious. He would slither into a room and own it within minutes, yet he would slink into your heart and remain forever.

My dad's name is "The Lizard."

This book is dedicated to him and the legacy of love, faith, and laughter he left behind. He set an example of a life well-lived in every aspect. He was a source of strength, light, and encouragement to all who knew and loved him. He is greatly missed by so many… especially Daddy's Little Girl.

ABC's
for Parents or Caregivers of Grievers

If you are the parent or caregiver of a grieving child, adolescent or young adult, it's important for you to be prepared as much as possible for the journey ahead.

Can I fix this?

As much as you would like, you cannot "fix" this situation for the child nor can you "fix" the child. It's important to know that heartache and grief cannot, and should not, be avoided. Those grieving should enter the pain and experience it, in order to recover from it.

Won't my child grow out of this?

Grief in children can arise anytime throughout the different developmental stages of growth and even into adulthood. If that grief is suppressed it may only rear itself in a more negative and detrimental way later on. So the griever is encouraged to embrace the sorrow and allow it for a time.

Will this go on forever?

In the beginning, this grief journey may feel all-consuming to everyone involved; it may seem as if it will always be overwhelming. However, if the child is allowed to thoroughly experience the loss, the grief will lose its dominance, then eventually decrease its force and take its place in the background.

"Children are often the forgotten grievers."
—David Kessler

The following ABC's are guidelines to parents and/or caregivers; but they are only suggestions because every grieving situation and every griever is different.

A	Allow the grief	N	Never give up
B	Be comforting	O	Observe disturbing behavior
C	Communication and Connection	P	Patience
D	Don't assume	Q	Questions answered
E	Empathize	R	Regular routines
F	Freedom of expression	S	Spiritual matters
G	Grieve together	T	Trustworthy
H	Help with identity crisis	U	Unfair and Unrealistic expectations
I	Include the child	V	Validate feelings
J	Just love	W	Withdrawal
K	Keep fun alive	X	eXpect the uneXpected
L	Live each day	Y	You are important
M	Mood swings	Z	Zest for the future

A **Allow the grief**: Allow young people to express their grief in their own way and in their own time. A child's grief can be more intense or drawn out than an adult's. This may be difficult for caregivers because of the desire to protect children from anything painful. Resist the temptation to shield them from the hurt and pain; a child's grief must be allowed.

B **Be comforting**: Ensure the griever you are there to take care of him. Use affection and kindness while consoling him as best you can. Reassure the child and give him hope. Be a good listener and ask how he would like to be comforted. Find out what makes him feel safe and what eases his pain.

C **Communication and Connection**: It is extremely important to keep the lines of communication open and stay connected to the child. Grieving can bring isolation, which can be a lonely and desolate place for a young person. Don't separate from a hurting child; stay connected to her even though you may be grieving yourself.

Be aware of what she is feeling and what is going on in her life. What is she doing? How is she processing the loss? What is she feeling? Is she communicating or expressing her feelings? Help children put their feelings into words. Make yourself available for positive communication and a true connection.

Don't just ask questions in passing; look at the child, giving your full attention and connecting with what you hear. Listen to what is said, even if it is uncomfortable.

Never force someone to talk, only encourage communication. Assure the griever you will be available to listen if you are needed.

Sometimes communication and connection can be made with absolutely no words. There are times when words just don't seem appropriate. However, you can still connect with a hug, pat on the back or a smile and communicate that you care and that she is valued.

D **Don't assume**: Every person and every grieving situation is different, so don't assume you know how the griever feels, and don't assume you know exactly what the griever needs. Each person's needs are different, especially those of children and young adults, so ask the child what his needs are instead of assuming.

E **Empathize**: Respond to the child with genuine concern and empathy. Recognize and, if you can, share her emotions. Always use compassion while talking and listening. Be sensitive to the feelings behind her words and actions. Help the griever through the journey with love and understanding.

F **Freedom of expression**: Accept the young griever unconditionally and support him as he expresses himself freely. Allow expression of emotions within boundaries so he doesn't hurt himself or others. This may be uncomfortable to see at times, but assure him that you will remain by his side. Young people, especially children, tend to express their grief in behavior. Be attentive that words may not always come easily for some grievers, and expression of feelings may be exhibited in other ways.

G **Grieve together**: Be careful not to isolate. Sometimes young grievers are alienated because they are being sheltered or it is assumed they are too young to understand. When death and tragedy strikes, even adults don't understand. So, allow young people to be a part of the family's grieving process.

H **Help with identity crisis**: Help maintain and develop the child's identity after the loss, especially in older children. The previous identity of the child may have been compromised and the roles may now be confused. A young girl may have felt pride in being "daddy's little girl", but after the loss of her father may feel that she no longer has that title. A young boy could have enjoyed being called the "little man" of the family, but after the death of a parent, separation, or divorce, he may feel he should be the "big man" now. Children can feel bewildered about all of the changes, their place in the family and what is expected of them. Because they may feel or think differently now, they could have a feeling of not knowing who they are anymore. Offer guidance and assurance while helping them redefine their roles and rediscover who they are.

I **Include the child**: Include the child in grief, future plans, and decisions where possible. Allow him to cry with you, have an input in the funeral preparations, or suggest plans to move forward in the situation. Try not to keep him away from family discussions. Communicate necessary information to the young griever. He needs to participate in the family loss and should not be left out. Also, share with the griever in the confrontation of pain and the process of recovery.

J **Just love**: When overwhelmed or confused, simply remember to love the child. As a parent or caregiver, you may become confused or even overwhelmed in your own grief. In those instances, just love. Don't worry about saying the right thing or having the correct response; it's more important that you show genuine love.

K **Keep fun alive**: Try to create opportunities for recreation, play, and laughter. This sounds impossible but is very important to the grieving child. Fun was a major part of the child's life prior to the loss, and it is important for her to engage in recreation as soon as she wants and feels able to. Encourage her to participate in creative expressions of her feelings. Fun is a part of "normalcy" and can be a vital part of recovery.

L **Live each day**: It is essential to demonstrate the importance of living life to the fullest. Live in the moment of each day and teach the child the value of life and our time here. Even though there will be painful times ahead, let the griever know that you can still find joy each day and appreciate the time you do have.

M **Mood swings**: Emotions and behaviors can be very volatile during this overwhelming time. It is not uncommon for young grievers to experience learning problems and trouble in school or social situations, even if they never have before.

Grief can bring difficulty in concentrating and paying attention, lack of focus, preoccupation with worry and loss, regression in behavior, shock, anger, isolation, confusion, depression, sleeping problems, physical symptoms, denial and guilt. The rush of these feelings and reactions can create mood swings at any time.

Allow your young person to talk freely about his feelings when he's having a bad time or worried, instead of acting out in bad behavior or withdrawal.

N **Never give up**: Never give up on a child and her ability to progress in the grief journey. Encourage her often and continually offer hope. It is vital that you never surrender in your journey so you can teach her about perseverance and pressing through the very difficult times.

O **Observe disturbing behavior**: It is crucial to recognize painful feelings and disturbing behaviors. Aggression, extreme withdrawal, depression, and suicidal thoughts are all behaviors that require immediate attention.

If disturbing words, thoughts or actions are causing concern, then notify the appropriate helping professionals and authority*. The child's safety is the utmost concern.

Do not hesitate in reporting alarming conduct. You must define the "fine line" of what is allowed and appropriate; your judgment and discernment is essential. Seek professional help when in doubt about unsettling behaviors.

If a child is in immediate danger, dial 911 for help. Otherwise, a list of helpful numbers and websites has been provided in the resources section of this book.

P **Patience**: Be patient with a griever. He may exhibit behavior contrary to what you are used to seeing from him. He may not act as he normally would, or he may say unusual things. He may become more quiet and withdrawn or may act out his confusion and pain. Reassure him of your support and love. Don't rush the grief process, because healing occurs at different rates. It is his journey, and you can best help him by demonstrating patience.

Q **Questions answered**: Answer a young person's questions honestly and age-appropriately. Talk openly and avoid using confusing words like "sleeping" or "gone away" when talking about death. Use straightforward terminology, but in terms she can understand. Be simplistic and factual when explaining the loss and details of the situation. Evading questions and creating secrecy can be even more disturbing and unsettling to the child. A direct but sensitive answer is usually best.

R **Regular routines**: Make an effort to keep as many routines as regular as possible. A consistent and structured environment can be very soothing and reassuring to a child in chaos. It is important to simplify your schedules and not overload the child, while trying to keep as much normalcy in his routine as you can.

S **Spiritual matters**: Spiritual concerns often arise during tragedy and loss. Share with young grievers reassuring beliefs of hope and the love of Jesus Christ, the Savior. Read Scriptures to children daily, or provide the older ones with a Bible they can read on their own. *The Holy Bible* is a source of encouragement, and reading the printed Word can give supernatural strength to the mourning. Words of life can soothe the aching soul and comfort those who read them. Also, encourage grieving children to pray and talk to God on their own.

T **Trustworthy**: Show grievers of all ages that you can be trusted to tell the truth. Be honest with your children. Young people are very intuitive and can sense when you're not telling the truth.

Demonstrate what you can about your feelings or details of situations. Share what you are feeling, good or bad, as needed, but be appropriate and use discernment in what you reveal.

Encourage the young griever to be truthful about her feelings and not just say what she thinks you want to hear. Be respectful and let her know you can be trusted with what she tells you.

U **Unfair or Unrealistic expectations**: Unfair expectations of a child can slow progress and create further setbacks. Sometimes it is insinuated, or children may feel, it is their responsibility to take on duties that are beyond their capabilities. Don't expect or allow your young person to take on inappropriate roles. Let him comfort others without assuming a "caregiver" role.

Also, don't have unrealistic expectations for the child's grief journey. Don't expect brief turmoil followed by a quick recovery. The duration of grief and the reaction to grief differs with each individual. The grief of any child is not exactly like yours, or others'; there's no "textbook" grief journey.

V **Validate feelings**: Listen to how the grieving child feels and let him know it's normal to feel the way he does. It is a very confusing time, and he may feel abnormal or out of control.

Let him know that grief is normal and that reactions to it can differ. Confirm his thoughts by letting him know you share some of the same ones.

W **Withdrawal**: Withdrawal may compound feelings of isolation and loss. Encourage the griever to communicate when feeling isolated. Some people may not want to share their feelings during this time, so let her know you are there to support her. Maybe a quiet hug or just your presence is needed. Be observant for signs that withdrawal might develop into a situation of concern.

X **eXpect the uneXpected**: The journey through grief is not mapped out; anything can happen or be said at anytime. Be prepared for out-of-control emotions, unusual feelings, strange actions and abnormal behavior. Grief is an intense feeling of pain that can be unpredictable. Being overwhelmed with so many confusing emotions can lead to thoughts and behaviors you never expected.

Y **You are important**: The young griever needs you and your love to help him through the difficult times. Your support is priceless. Take care of yourself and make sure your own needs are met. You are valuable, so treat yourself with love and kindness.

Z **Zest for the future**: Be enthusiastic for the future and the "new normal" that is to be created. Even though the pain may be dominant now, let children know there is expectation for a joyful life ahead. Encourage young grievers and fill them with hope that they will progress and feel better someday. Give them confidence to trust themselves and God for a happy and exciting future.

Stories of Grief and Loss

Dealing with the questions and emotions following significant loss or the death of a loved one.

These stories are about the various emotions and many questions that follow a major loss or death of someone special. No matter where the grief comes from, the separation and loss can be traumatic and confusing.

Listen in on the conversations in these four stories. Perhaps you, or the person you are reading to, will identify with a character, situation or emotion. Children of all ages, even grown children, can relate to the feelings and struggles, in each of the accounts.

Read on and let these stories open the door for a journey of grief and recovery.

The stories:

"I Just Want My Daddy Back!" is the story of a young child's confusing emotions and endless questions following the death of his father.

"Saying Good-bye" addresses the loss of a preteen's beloved pet that had grown old and ill. It's difficult to let go, even knowing ahead of time that a loved one is dying.

"No Tragedies in a Perfect World" is about a teenager's reaction to loss after her two friends die suddenly in a traffic accident.

"Just Gone" is the story of a young family torn apart by divorce and an unexpected move. Grief can be experienced without death. Loss can come from divorce, separation, moving, or the loss of stability, routine, family unit, and friends. A change in "normal" life can be difficult for young people, especially those grieving.

I Just Want My Daddy Back!

I want my daddy back!

Where is he? Where did he go? Doesn't he miss me? Doesn't he want to see me? Why can't I see him anymore? I just want my daddy back!

You tell me that he died.

You say that he lives in Heaven now, but if he's dead, how can he live somewhere else?

You tell me that I can't see him now, but I can see him again when I get to Heaven… I don't even know where Heaven is!

You tell me if I just close my eyes and open my heart I can see my daddy. Well I don't see him. He's not here! I'm so confused.

Momma, I just want my daddy back!

Grandma told me that Daddy was in a better place now… but I thought our place was the best place ever!

My Sunday School teacher told me "there are no tears in Heaven." How can Daddy miss me as much as I miss him and not cry? Maybe he doesn't even remember me.

My friend's big sister told me "God does everything for a reason." Did God want my daddy to die? What reason would be good enough to take my daddy away and make me this sad?

I get so sad that my tummy hurts. I don't feel like playing with my friends, or even riding my bike when I get this sad.

I sometimes get so sad that I get mad! I want to punch my pillow and stomp my feet!!

At other times, I get so sad that all I can do is cry, cry, cry…

And sometimes I'm so sad, I can't even cry at all. I think that is when my heart hurts the most.

Oh, I just want my daddy back!

You say he's happy where he's at now, but I thought he was happy here. It doesn't seem fair that Daddy is happy without me... because I am so sad without him.

How can I ever be happy again when my heart hurts so bad?

Uncle Gary said that "time heals all wounds." How long is "time"? Will it be here by tomorrow, or next year, or will it take the rest of my life? Can we hurry "time" up?

I just want to close my eyes very tight and when I open them, then "time" will be here to make it all better.

Oh, Momma, I just want my daddy back.

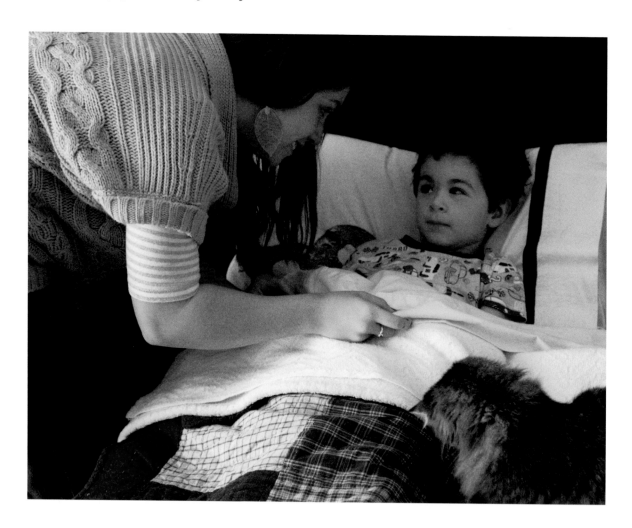

I miss him too, sweetheart... but I can't bring Daddy back.
Believe me, Tory; I would if I could.
I can't even answer all of your questions. I have questions too.
However, what I can do is hold you tight, love you with all my heart and pray for you. That is exactly what I am going to do once you snuggle into your bed and close your eyes.

Tory, Tory… wake up.

Huh?

Don't be afraid. I have come to talk with you.
I understand you are very hurt and have a lot of questions about your dad.

Who are you? Are you an angel?

Well, not exactly. Do you want to talk for a while?

Sure, I guess so... but I don't think it will help. No one can answer all my questions.

I will try.

My daddy died. Can you bring him back?

No, Tory, your dad has left this world for good and he won't be coming back here. Actually, your dad didn't die. He is still very much alive and doing perfectly well, only he is in a different place.

Can I see him?

Yes, someday you will, but not yet.

I don't understand. Everyone told me that my daddy died; even Momma said he was dead! Why would they lie to me?

They didn't lie to you, my dear child, they only told you what they understood. You see, Tory, we all have a spirit inside of us, the part that is really who we are. Our spirit lives inside our body while we live here on Earth. Whenever it is time for us to leave this world, only the spirit goes. Do you understand?

I think so.

The body is left behind and stays here because we don't need it in our new home.

So Daddy didn't really die, only his body did?

That's right, your daddy never died for a second. His spirit just left his body and went to the wonderful place he lives now. Your dad is in a beautiful new home called Heaven and he made it there just fine. Your grandpa was there to welcome him, along with his other friends and relatives that were already there.

He's really there?

Yes, it was a huge celebration when he arrived.

Like a party?

Like the biggest, most awesome party you could ever imagine!

I wish I could have been there.

Don't worry; there will be a big celebration when you get to Heaven too.

I don't even know where Heaven is. I don't think I could get there by myself. What if I get lost?

My dear, I will get you to Heaven. You just trust me and follow me. I promise you won't be lost. Let me guide your life here and then I will lead you to the place where you will live with me, my Father and your dad forever.

Are you Jesus?

Yes, Tory, I am.

My daddy told me about you.

Yes, I know. Because your dad believed in me and loved me here, he lives with us in Heaven now.

So Heaven is real?

Yes, it is. I have even walked with your dad there. He loves you and your mother very much and I see why you miss him so.

Does he miss me?

He is always with you, Tory, and you are with him. You know it was your dad's job to take care of you and look after your needs while he was here.

Yeah, he was always there when I needed him.

Even now, it is part of his job to continue that. Your father is like a guardian angel to you. He is still watching over you and he still loves you, just like your Heavenly Father does.

You mean God?

Exactly, Tory. You are one of God's children and He loves you more than you can imagine.

Then why did He take my daddy?

God never wants His children to be troubled or sad but that does happen here sometimes. Everyone must leave this Earth; some leave earlier than others, which makes the ones left behind very sad.

I know. I'm very, very sad.

God loves you so much that He wants to comfort you and be with you during these hard times. He wants to help you feel better. Just remember, God will always be with you, Tory, and you will never be alone.

Is He here right now?

Yes, He is. All you have to do is call to Him.

Do I need a special phone to talk to God?

No Tory, just call out His name and begin talking with Him. That is what prayer is.

Will I be able to see God when I talk to Him?

Probably not, but you will be able to feel Him. You will know He is there with you.

Are you sure God can help me?

Of course He can, although it is going to take some time and effort.

But I'm so sad my heart hurts!

As sad as you are, you have to keep trying and keep living just like your mother, grandma and all the others that miss your dad.

I don't want to do this! I don't want to go through this hard stuff! I just want my daddy back!

I understand, Tory. I also had to walk through painful times and God helped me through, just as He will help you. It will get easier and hurt less as you continue on with your life here. Then someday, you will see your father, your Heavenly Father and me.

I want to go see my daddy now.

No, Tory, you still have so much life to live before then. You have new experiences to be a part of, new people to meet, new places to go and lots more fun to have.

How can God fix it so I can ever have fun and play again?

God will go with you through this painful time. You can do this because He will give you power and courage. With each passing day, week and season, you will become stronger because God gives us the strength even when we feel weak and scared.

I just don't think I can do all that without my daddy, especially the having fun part.

Yes. Yes, you can! Your dad had his experiences in this world; some were fun and some were not so fun, but he loved life! Now he wants you to do the same.

Really?

Yes, he doesn't want to see you sad and brokenhearted. He wants to see you enjoying your time here with your mother and your friends.

But if I'm not sad, my daddy might think I don't miss him.

No, that's not right. Your dad knows that you will always love him and that you'll also miss him. However, he wants to see you smile again. He wants to hear that silly laugh you have and he wants others to hear it too.

He does?

Your dad wants you to remember the things he told you and recall the times you spent together. He wants you to talk about him with a joyful heart. Tory, your daddy wants a part of him to live in you... but most of all he wants you to live!

I can do that.

If you live your life full of love, it will help ease your pain. Also, live your life full of hope. There is a hope of a stronger tomorrow and a happier day after.

So it will get better?

Yes, my dear, it will. Expect to see God's miracles in your life every day because He will be there helping you. Live big and live for Me! Not only will you get better, but you will be blessed also.

Do you really think so?

I know so.

Thanks for coming here and talking to me.

You are so very welcome.

I love you, Jesus.

I have always loved you, Tory.

Tory, wake up.
Wake up, sweetheart, it's time to get ready for school.

Momma, Momma… today is going to be different! Today is going to be better; I just know it.

What do you mean, dear?

We're not alone, Momma. We can make it through this together and we can be happy even though Daddy is not here. We will laugh again, you'll see. It's okay to be happy; Daddy would like that.

Just close your eyes and open your heart… do you see Daddy? He's smiling at us! Do you feel him?

Yes, dear, I think I do.

Hey, Momma… let's go for a bike ride after school today.

That sounds great, honey. I would love to do that with you.

Saying Good-bye

That was the hardest thing I have ever had to do. I said good-bye, but I still can't let go. He looked so sad and helpless. I hope he wasn't scared. I wonder if he knew he was dying. Are you sure we did the right thing, Dad?

Yes, son. Danny had to be put to sleep.

Why do people say that, anyway? He's not sleeping; he's dead.

I know, Blake, it's just a phrase people use.

Well, I'll tell you, it doesn't feel like we did the right thing. I just don't know.

We did what we had to do because Danny was a very old and extremely sick dog.

I guess I do understand that. You're right; we had to do something, because I saw him getting thinner and weaker. I know he was in pain.

He hadn't wanted to play fetch or race to the mailbox in a long time. Lately, he's just been sleeping a lot. It was so hard seeing him sick like that. He didn't act like himself before he died. He didn't look like himself, either.

I kind of lost him even before he died. We couldn't do the same things as we did before, but I thought he would get better; I really did. I even prayed every night that God would make him well again.

I know, I heard you praying. God heard you, too.

Well, I'm mad about that, cause if God heard me, why didn't He heal Danny? He was such a good dog; he didn't deserve to suffer. Why didn't God heal him?

I don't know, son. Now and then, bad and hurtful things happen. Even though we pray, sometimes illness or death comes before we are ready. I don't understand it all, either. But you know we did all we could to make Danny comfortable before he died. You were with him until the end.

I know; he died while I was saying good-bye. Do you think he heard me? What if he didn't hear me?

Danny knew that you loved him. You were always there for him; you guys were best friends, and Danny knew that. You didn't have to say it with your words; you showed it through your love.

He was my best friend, and now nothing will ever be the same. You gave me Danny on my first birthday and he's been by my side ever since I can remember. I couldn't take a step without him. Do you remember that we would stay outside playing catch till dark? He loved the grounders.

He was there when I fell out of the tree and when I crashed my bike into the picnic table. He's the one who went for help both times. Remember? We did everything together. We played, shared snacks, took walks, slept together...

You two even took baths together!

Yeah, we're buddies; I mean we *were* buddies. I'm gonna be so lonely now that he's gone. How can I ever replace him? I can never love another dog as much as Danny. He was the best!

He was awesome and no other dog will ever replace Danny. But I'm sure as time goes on, you will be able to love another dog. He wouldn't take Danny's place; he would just be a new friend. You have too much love in that heart of yours to keep it all to yourself.

I don't know, Dad. If I ever did love another dog, I would be scared. I would be scared that if he ever died someday, I would feel this bad all over again. I can't ever do this again; it hurts too much.

Yes, Blake, love is a risk, but it's worth it. Just think of all the happy memories. I know you are hurting now, but all the good feelings Danny left with you certainly outweigh the bad ones.

But my heart hurts so much and my stomach aches deep down inside.

When the vet told us a few weeks ago that Danny was going to die soon, I felt like someone hit me in the gut with a baseball bat–I couldn't breathe. I didn't think anything could feel that bad inside, but now that he's gone; it even hurts worse. I didn't think that was possible.

Since I knew Danny was going to die, I thought it would make it easier when he did. I sort of thought I would be prepared, but I was wrong.

It's always hard saying good-bye to those we love, whether they are still here or already gone. Even after saying good-bye, we have the process of letting go.

I don't want to let go of Danny! When he was dying, I held on to him so tight, maybe even too tight. I can't let go! He was too special to me.

I don't mean you have to let go of the memories of Danny; they are forever with you. I'm talking about letting go of the pain, the fear, the anger, and the blame…things like that; the hurtful things.

I don't know how to do that, Dad. I'm so confused about it all. I've never felt like this.

Son, I don't know what to do, either, but together we can figure some things out. I know you have lost your best friend and I'll do what I can to help you. I feel that talking like this will help, and I also feel that talking to God will help.

I already tried that when Danny was alive, and it didn't help.

Blake, you have to understand that just because things don't work out like we want them to, doesn't mean God isn't listening. I don't have all the answers, but He does. Even if He doesn't tell us all the answers, He is still there. God loves you so much; you are His child, too. He wants to help you feel better and be happy again—just like I do.

I'm so sorry you are hurting and so is He. I think God wants you to reach out and talk to him again so He can help your pain. He will give you strength and courage; He will also help straighten out all of those confused feelings you have.

I sure hope God can help, cause I'm so mixed up right now, I can't even cry. I feel guilty about not crying after losing my best friend.

Don't feel guilty, son. Everyone mourns in a different way.

What do you mean by "mourn"?

Mourning is just how you express your grief and sadness. It's how you deal with your pain. There is no correct or proper way to get through grief. This is your grief and you have to work through it in your own way.

There are so many different ways to feel, and even more ways to show it. For you, the tears may come later, or maybe not. You may feel a different way each day or feel a bunch of different ways all at the same time! That's why it's important for us to talk when you need to and express your hurt and confusion when you need to.

Thanks, Dad. You are right about the talking. It has helped just talking with you now. I'm glad I can come to you and you will listen.

You're welcome. I love you and I'm always here for you and remember… God is, too. He also loves you and He will listen to you and be here to help you through this.

Do you think God will still listen to me even though I'm mad at Him?

Absolutely. He knows your heart and He sees that it's hurting right now. Don't give up on God, because He will never give up on you.

That's good to know. Hey Dad… will you help me finish the cross I was making for Danny's grave?

Of course I will. I've seen what you've done so far and I know Danny would be proud.

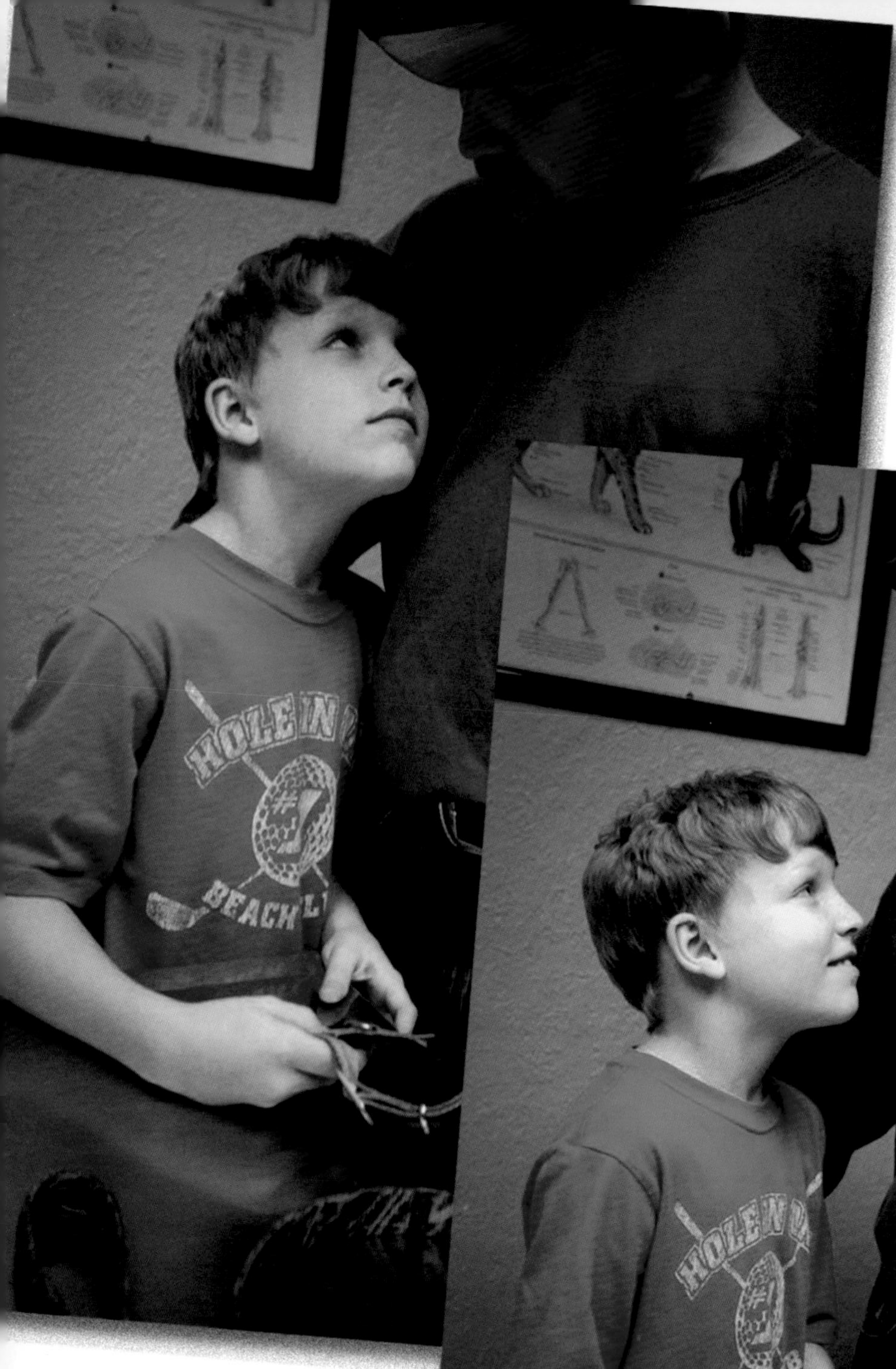

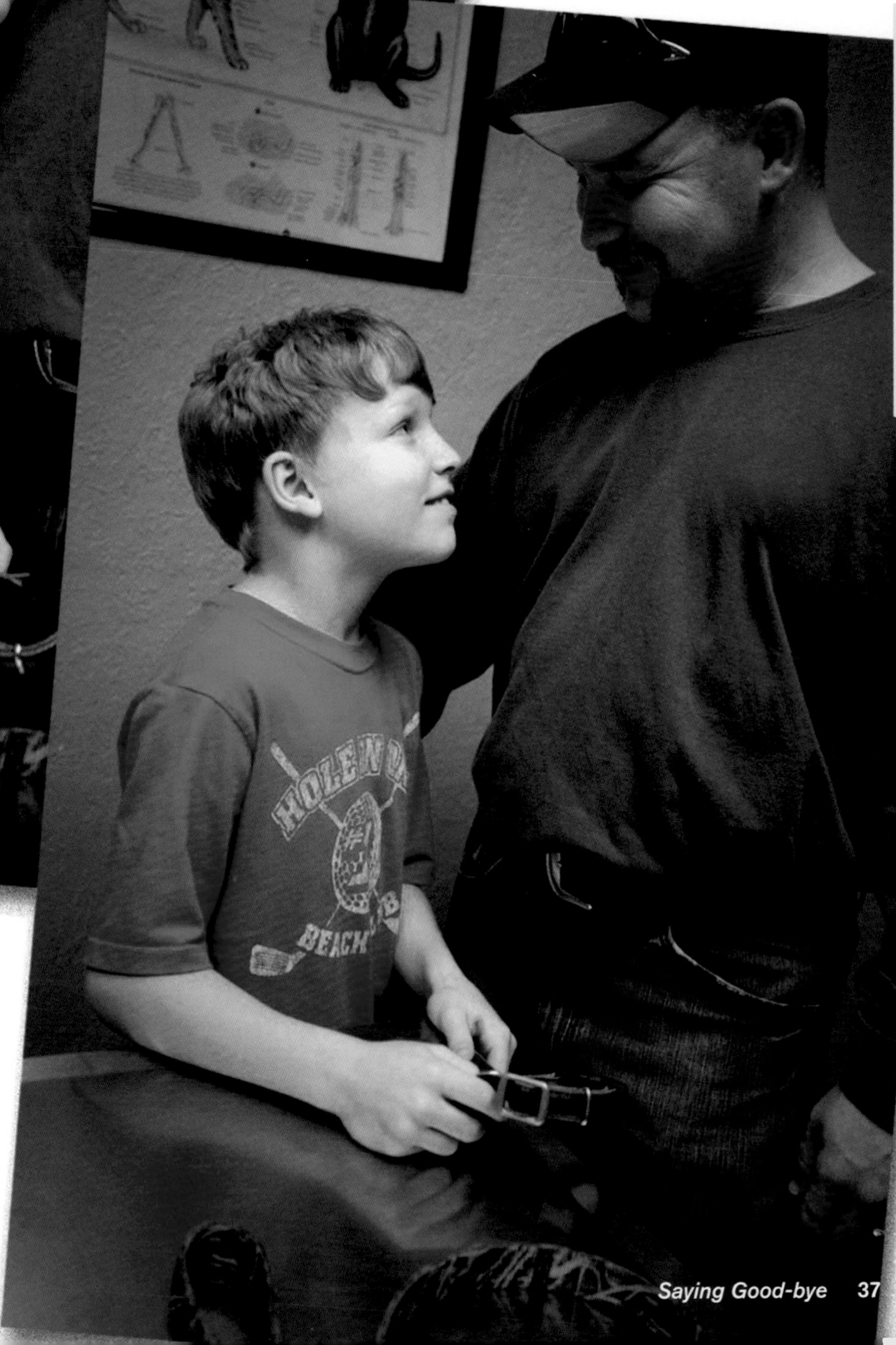

No Tragedies in a Perfect World

I don't think I can do it. I can't go into the funeral, Grandma. I can't see my friends like that… so lifeless. What if I burst out crying and I can't stop? I'm so upset, I feel sick. I might even throw up or pass out! I can't do it. I just can't!

You don't have to go in there, Jenny, if you think you can't. However, I personally feel you are strong enough to be a part of this.

Grandma, I just can't believe this is happening. Just a few days ago Ashley and I were shopping for our prom dresses. We had so much fun; I know we tried on a hundred. Zach even had his tux all picked out, the one with the long tail and top hat.

Now they're gone! How is that even possible? One minute we're making plans for the biggest night of our lives and in one split second they're gone… their lives are over! That's just too big for me to grasp. How could two people so funny, so caring, so full of life… be dead?

I know it's a lot to deal with right now, Jen. You're still in shock.

I *am* shocked! I *am* shocked, devastated and angry! How could someone get drunk and then try to drive a car? That stupid decision cost me my two best friends and ruined my life forever!

I know you can't see it now, sweetheart, but you will get through this.

Well, they won't! It's not fair; they didn't deserve to die. How could God let this happen, anyway? It's just not fair!

No, dear, it's not fair, but things happen in this life that we don't understand. In a perfect world there would be no hurting, sadness, illness or accidents. There would be no car wrecks in a perfect world… there would be no tragedies in a perfect world.

I guess that perfect world you're talking about would be Heaven, because it's sure not here. I hope Heaven is real; I need to believe that it's real. It helps me to think that Ashley and Zach just didn't cease to exist.

I need to believe that they are in a great place right now, laughing and living it up on some streets of gold or something. It makes me feel better to imagine them in a place like Heaven doin' some kind of angel stuff.

Can't you see Ashley singing in the choir? She loves being in the spotlight… or loved being in the spotlight. I don't even know if my best friend *is* or *was*!

Oh, Jenny, I believe your friend was here on Earth but now is in Heaven.

Grandma, I'm not sure what I believe anymore. My thoughts and feelings are all over the place. I just can't seem to get a grip on how I feel, or what is real.

That's okay, Jen, you'll sort it out in time, but right now the funeral is starting. Do you think you can go in?

Yes, Grandma, I need to do this. I guess it's what you call "closure," but I'm not sure I want to do this.

I'm so tired. I'm just drained. I never knew facing death could be this hard. I can't eat, I can't sleep; I can't concentrate on anything.

All I can think about is the accident and the fact that I'll never see my friends again. I'll never talk to them… ever. No more visits, phone calls, not even a text.

It won't sink in; I don't want it to. We were just making plans for college. Now I don't even care if I go. I feel so alone and empty inside, Grandma. You know that Ashley and I were best friends since the first day of kindergarten. We've always done everything together.

How am I supposed to go on with my life without her? I'm so hurt and confused; I'm just not the same anymore. Why couldn't I have just died with them?

…No, Grandma, I really don't want to die, I just don't know how to live with this much pain….

No, I don't think time will help; but who knows? Thanks anyway, Grandma.

I love you too.

God, if you're there, please help me! I'm going crazy here, I need some help!

I'm here, Jennifer. Come over here and sit with me.

God, is that you?... Where are you?

What is this place? Is this Heaven?

This is one of my favorite spots to come and sit quietly. Won't you join me?

Yes, I will. Are you God?

I am the Son of God. He has sent me here for your sake. God sees that your heart is broken and has heard your cries.

Thank God… literally. So how is God going to fix this nightmare? My friends are dead and so many people are hurt because of it, especially their families… and me. Tell me the plan to fix it all.

There is no plan to reverse what has been done, Jennifer. The plan is for you to grieve the loss of your friends and rebuild your life without them here.

No! You are Jesus, the Son of God Almighty! Fix this! Fix this now! Tell God to fix it!

Jennifer, you live in a world where each person has free will, and with that comes great responsibility. The person driving the car that killed your friends had a choice that evening. His choice to overindulge in alcohol, then try to drive home was a decision he will regret for the rest of his life.

Good! I hate him for that! He should suffer… I hate him!

I know that you are angry, but at some point you must let that go and forgive the man for his wrong choice.

Wrong choice? He is a sinner and a murderer! Punish him for what he did!

Jennifer, laying blame, judging, and becoming bitter will only keep you from your peace.

I will never have peace again. I just want to wake up from this horrible nightmare and have my friends back… back here the way it was.

They are not coming back and things will not be as they were before. Nevertheless, peace will come again and joy will return. But first, there is a journey you must take. You will experience many emotions along the way. However, you will not journey alone.

You talk about a journey… I can't even think about getting through the rest of the day. I can't do this. My thoughts are twisted and I can't think straight. I don't even know who I am anymore!

That is why I am here, to reassure you and to offer you comfort. I want you to know how much God loves you and will not forsake you. He will be here with you through every tear, every angry fit, and all of the confusion. Pour your despair out on Him. He will love you through it all and so will I.

I don't think so. I don't feel so "holy" or close to God right now. I don't want to forgive and I'm even mad at God for letting this all happen.

Even though you are angry and don't feel close to God, He is still close to you. He will uphold you and love you through your pain. His love never fails and never changes. He will never leave you, nor will I.

Your faith will help you heal.

But I did have faith. I had faith that if I was a good person and lived a good life, everything would be okay.

Jennifer, I want you to live well and live for me because you love me. That is why I died for you. Your belief and your love for me assures your eternal life with your Heavenly Father and me. However, it does not eliminate the trials and pain experienced here in this world. Remember the free will? Those actions have consequences.

The pain of free will is too much to bear.

You need to face your pain, feel the grief of your loss and mourn as your heart leads.

What if I can't deal with this much pain? I feel so broken and helpless.

You will be fine because God will strengthen you and help heal your broken heart. It will be difficult at times but you must keep trying.

How do you know that God will really help me?

Keep your faith and trust in Me, Jennifer. Lean on Me and talk to Me; My spirit is always with you.

I don't have faith that I'll ever be the same. Will I ever be the same?

No, my child, you won't. You will be a wiser and stronger version of your former self. As time progresses, you will also progress in your healing. Be willing to let go of the blame, release your heart to forgiveness and redirect the negative energy you feel. When you do this, you will see yourself returning even sooner. You will become a stronger person than you were before.

That just seems impossible right now.

I know it does, but your strength will come. Trust in Me, Jennifer. You will never forget your friends or the time you had with them. They are a part of you forever, though the pain is not. You will pass through the anger, heartache and desolation of losing them.

Jesus...

Yes, Jennifer?

There is one more thing that bothers me. If heaven is real, how can I be sure that Ashley is there? Zach knew You, but I don't know if Ashley did. We never talked about it... I mean, You. Can you tell me if she is in Heaven?

Ashley is a fine girl, and like you, has a beautiful spirit; however, it is the Father that knows the beliefs and state of each heart. He is full of endless mercy and grace.

It's just without the hope of her life continuing on after death, I don't think I can survive this. I can't even imagine Ashley and Zach not living someplace where they're happy.

If it is that important to you, Jennifer, maybe you should share your love of Me with more people.

I don't know how to do that. That's why I never talked to Ashley about You.

All you have to do is love people the way I showed you and the words will come. My light will shine through you. Open your heart; the Holy Spirit will guide you when you talk about Me to others.

I guess I can do that.

I will be with you in those circumstances, and I will be with you during your grief journey. It isn't going to be easy, but I have heard it said that "All things are possible with"…well, you know.

Yes, I really do know that You make all things possible. I had faith in You before, and now I will also trust You. Thanks for taking the time to talk to me and thanks for being with me.

I love you, Jennifer. By the way… Ashley says to wear the red dress to prom.

I had the craziest dream last night. I think it was a dream, but it seemed so real. After I woke up this morning, I just felt better. I don't know how to describe it, Grandma, my gut still aches and my heart still hurts but it's better... I guess I feel different because I have hope.

Yes, Grandma, hope is a good thing. I think I'll try to use some of this mixed-up energy I have and put it to good use. For quite some time now, I have wanted to do something that helps people. Maybe I'll warn kids about the dangers of drunk driving or start a prayer group after school. Today, I think I'll make a scrapbook from my photos for Zach's parents and Ashley's parents. Maybe later I can get some friends together to plant a tree on the school campus in their honor. I've got lots of ideas... and tomorrow, I'm going to buy that gorgeous red prom dress.

Just Gone

What do you mean we're going to move? First you tell us that you and Dad are getting a divorce and now you tell us *this*! Why do we have to move?

> I think that it would be better for all of us to move back near your grandparents. They will be able to help out since your dad isn't here.

But Dad is here—he didn't die! He just lives across town!

> I know you don't understand, but this is for the best.

How could you ruin our lives like this? We are your kids, how could you do this to us? How could you move us halfway across the country?!

> Please don't be angry with me. I'm not doing any of this to hurt you; I'm trying to make things better for all of us.

But Mom, how could this be for the best? Do you want me to be an emotional wreck for the rest of my life?

> Of course not. I don't want to see you, your brother or sister upset.

Well, we are going to be! Is that really how you want us to grow up, away from our home and without a dad? What about the little kids? They especially need a dad!

> You won't grow up without your father; you just won't see him as often. I know it's not how you want it, but sometimes things happen and life doesn't turn out how we planned. We don't always understand it all. I know it's hard, but I believe I'm doing the right thing, even if it doesn't seem like it.

I don't believe this is best. I don't want to go! This is hurting me so bad I can't stand it! You both are ruining my life with the stupid divorce and now this move!

> I'm so sorry, honey.

I'm going to my room… I need to be by myself.

Why are you crying, Angie?

You wouldn't understand… but thanks for checking on me.

I may be little, but I still want to help.

I know you do, Alex, but you can't help me right now… nobody can. Why don't you go take care of Amanda – she is the sister that probably needs you more.

Okay, Angie, I will.

Knock-knock, can I come in?

Hey, Aunt Joni. I heard you were coming over. Sorry I'm not myself, but I just got hit with some more bad news.

Your mom told me about the move. Is that why you've been crying?

Yes, everything's a mess. I am so mad right now. Dad moved out and now Mom is moving us away from him and our entire life. How could they do this to us?

Did you ever think she is doing what she thinks is best? She's trying to do what will benefit the family the most.

Well, she did tell me that, but how is taking me away from my dad, my school, my friends and my house going to help me? She's taking everything from me; from all of us!

I know you must be hurting pretty bad right now, but your mom is hurting, too.

Then why is she doing this? She doesn't have to move us.

It was a hard decision, but she feels that she needs to do this. She thinks under the circumstances, it is the right option. Don't you think the divorce and this move is hard on your mom, too? She has lost her marriage and is leaving her job, her friends and her church family, too. This is difficult for both of your parents.

I guess I never really thought of how it was upsetting them.

Sometimes it's difficult to think about how things are affecting others when you are hurting so much.

I know everybody is hurt. I feel even worse for Alex and Amanda. They are really too young to understand it all. They probably think we are going on some great adventure. They have no idea that life as we knew it is over... just gone. Exactly like Dad... just gone.

Things change, honey. I know that's hard for you; but have you thought that maybe the little kids are right? Maybe you could turn this into an adventure, too.

What kind of adventure would it be without Dad, away from our home? That sounds like a disaster, not an adventure!

You need to think positively. Moving to a new town with your brother, sister and your mom can be a new beginning for a different life. Different doesn't have to be bad. You'll be able to see your grandparents more, and you'll meet new friends in your new neighborhood. Change and new things can be good. You can become even stronger as a family if you all commit and work together.

But I don't want a new beginning. I want my old life back with Dad here!

You know life has a way of changing. It gives us the unexpected and the unplanned sometimes.

Life didn't do this; Mom and Dad did!

Your parents make decisions with your needs in mind, but things don't always work out as you planned. And then you have to do something different. Sometimes we can't do anything about the things that happen in life. However, we can control our reactions to those changes.

How can I change how terrible all this feels? It hurts so much for us to leave Dad behind. How could I ever stop missing him?

Angie, you will always love your dad and want to be with him; that won't change. His love for you won't change, either. Even though you won't see him as often, he will always love you and be there for you. He will always be your dad. You can keep in touch with him as much as you like, and he told me that he would come as often as he could to see you kids. You have to trust that everything will be all right.

I don't think I trust anything or anyone right now.

I have something for you. I was going to give it to you on your birthday, but I think you need it now.

What is this? You're giving me a Bible with my name on it?

Yes, that is your very own Bible. This book helped me through some very hard times in my life. I know you feel there is nothing you can trust right now, but I assure you, the words in this book are trustworthy. Believe me, God wants you and this family to feel better. He wants you all to be happy and feel complete again. He also wants to heal your hurts; it says so in here.

How can a book written so long ago really help me today? Does it say anything in here about moms and dads divorcing and turning their kids' lives upside down?

This book is full of encouraging words and stories of overcoming hard times. There are promises of God written in here, promises that he makes with those who love Him and trust Him. He will comfort you, strengthen you and bring you out of the dark, painful places and into a joyful place. He will teach you about forgiveness, restoration, hope, and love through His son Jesus Christ. It's all in here. Read it for yourself.

I don't even know where to start; it's a very big book.

Well, you could start at the beginning, or you could start with the verses I wrote down for you.

Do you really think it will make a difference?

I am certain this book and God's love will help you through these difficult times. The more you read, the more you will understand just how much He loves you. God sent His Son to this earth for us, so Jesus also knows how it feels to move away from a Father. As you will see, His Father's love never changed.

I'm starting to feel a little better just talking about it. Maybe I will read more about Jesus and His Father and see what happens.

Here are a few of the scriptures that helped me through my very difficult times. I know God will give you the same comfort, strength and hope He gave me.

Love, Aunt Joni

OLD TESTAMENT

Job 36:15 *But those who suffer he delivers in their suffering; he speaks to them in their affliction.*

Psalm 9:9-10 *The Lord is a refuge for the oppressed, a stronghold in times of trouble. Those who know your name will trust in you, for you, Lord have never forsaken those who seek you.*

Psalm 16:8 *I have set the Lord always before me. Because he is at my right hand, I will not be shaken.*

Psalm 22:5 *They cried to you and were saved; in you they trusted and were not disappointed.*

Psalm 23:4 *Even though I walk through the valley of the shadow of death, I will fear no evil, for you are with me; your rod and your staff, they comfort me.*

Psalm 27:1 *The Lord is my light and my salvation-whom shall I fear? The Lord is the stronghold of my life—of whom shall I be afraid?*

Psalm 27:14 *Wait for the Lord; be strong and take heart and wait for the Lord.*

Psalm 32:7 *You are my hiding place; you will protect me from trouble and surround me with songs of deliverance.*

Psalm 48:14 *For this God is our God for ever and ever; he will be our guide even to the end.*

Psalm 50:15 *...and call upon me in the day of trouble; I will deliver you, and you will honor me.*

Psalm 55:16-17 *But I call to God, and the Lord saves me. Evening, morning and noon I cry out in distress, and he hears my voice.*

Psalm 56:3-4 *When I am afraid, I will trust in you. In God, whose word I praise, in God I trust; I will not be afraid. What can mortal man do to me?*

Psalm 62:8 *Trust in him at all times, O people; pour out your hearts to him, for God is our refuge.*

Psalm 71:5 *…for you have been my hope, O Sovereign Lord, my confidence since my youth.*

Psalm 91:11 *For he will command his angels concerning you to guard you in all your ways.*

Psalm 119:50 *My comfort in my suffering is this: Your promise preserves my life.*

Psalm 119:107 *I have suffered much; reserve my life, O Lord, according to your word.*

Psalm 144:7 *Reach down your hand from on high; deliver me and rescue me…*

Isaiah 12:2 *Surely God is my salvation; I will trust and not be afraid. The Lord, the Lord, is my strength and my song; he has become my salvation.*

Isaiah 30:18 *Yet the Lord longs to be gracious to you; he rises to show you compassion. For the Lord is a God of justice. Blessed are all who wait for him!*

Isaiah 35:10 *Gladness and joy will overtake them, and sorrow and sighing will flee away.*

Lamentations 3:23 *They are new every morning; great is your faithfulness.*

Nahum 1:7 *The Lord is good, a refuge in times of trouble. He cares for those who trust in him.*

NEW TESTAMENT

Matthew 28:20 *(Jesus said) "And surely I am with you always, to the very end of the age."*

Ephesians 1:3 *Praise be to the God and Father of our Lord Jesus Christ, who has blessed us in the heavenly realms with every spiritual blessing in Christ.*

Hebrews 6:19 *We have this hope as an anchor for the soul, firm and secure.*

Hebrews 11:1 *Now faith is being sure of what we hope for and certain of what we do not see.*

James 1:2-5 *Consider it pure joy, my brothers, whenever you face trials of many kinds, because you know that the testing of your faith develops perseverance. Perseverance must finish its work so that you may be mature and complete, not lacking anything. If any of you lacks wisdom, he should ask God, who gives generously to all without finding fault, and it will be given to him.*

James 1:12 *Blessed is the man who perseveres under trial, because when he has stood the test, he will receive the crown of life that God has promised to those who love him.*

1 Peter 2:24 *He himself bore our sins in his body on the tree, so that we might die to sins and live for righteousness, by his wounds you have been healed.*

Activities for Your Grief Journey

1. Recognizing Your Losses
2. Reacting to Loss
3. Grief Stages
4. Identify Your Support System
5. Allowing the Grief and Pain
6. Hole in the Heart
7. Open and Honest
8. Angry Moments
9. Forgiveness
10. Pray
11. Fears Go Away!
12. "What-ifs" and Regrets
13. Ask "Why?"
14. Letting Go
15. Take Care of Yourself
16. The Sound of Music
17. Remember
18. Crying Time
19. Detours
20. What is Normal?
21. Gratitude List
22. Power of Positive Thinking
23. Be Creative
24. Sleep Tight
25. The Cookie Jar
26. Giving and Receiving
27. Treasure Chest
28. Space Invaders
29. Sweet Dreams or Nightmares?
30. Living Memorial
31. Stay Active
32. Holidays and Special Days
33. Acceptance
34. Saying Good-bye
35. Writing Your Own Obituary
36. Setting New Goals
37. Dance Like No One is Watching
38. Helping Another Griever
39. Smile
40. Have Fun!

Recognizing Your Losses

Each time we experience grief, we may be reminded of previous losses. This is normal, and although it may be painful, it actually can be helpful.

It may seem odd to intentionally think about past hurts, but **reviewing the course your grief has taken in the past will help you with your present pain**.

Here is the process that can help:

1. Identify the losses throughout your life, not just the most recent one. Many different kinds of losses can affect you deeply. They may be devastating losses or smaller ones that still made you feel bad.

2. Think about how you survived the trauma and how you dealt with the pain at the time. Be encouraged from your past recoveries, or start working through any remaining hurts.

Remember, not all losses have to do with death. Here are some examples of other losses:

* **Separation**

* **Divorce**

* **Moving**

* **Disability** after an illness or accident

* **Loss** of property (something important lost, destroyed, or stolen)

* **Loss** of relationships or love

* **Loss** of security, freedom, self-esteem, confidence, trust, hopes and dreams

---

Pray... *for healing the pain of all the losses in your life.*

Helpful Scriptures:

Psalm 147:3 *He (God) heals the brokenhearted and binds up their wounds.*

Romans 15:13 *May the God of hope fill you with all joy and peace as you trust in him, so that you may overflow with hope by the power of the Holy Spirit.*

Psalm 55:22 *Cast your cares on the Lord and he will sustain you.*

John 16:33 *(Jesus said) "I have told you these things, so that in me you may have peace. In this world you will have trouble. But take heart! I have overcome the world."*

"One often calms one's grief by recounting it."
—Pierre Corneille

Reacting to Loss

Individuals vary a great deal in how they react to each type of loss. **There's no "correct" way to react, and there is no right or wrong way to feel**.

What are some of the reactions you have felt since experiencing your major loss? Check the box by the words that describe what you have experienced and how you have felt. Add some of your own words. Talk about how you feel concerning these reactions, or write about them in your journal.

☐ Distressed	☐ Compassion
☐ Angry	☐ Isolation/Alone
☐ Sad	☐ Lost
☐ Overwhelmed	☐ Headache
☐ Relieved	☐ Out of Control
☐ Shock	☐ Confused
☐ Fear	☐ Regret
☐ Crying	☐ Doubtful
☐ Disbelief	☐ Helpless
☐ Numbness	☐ Hateful
☐ Stomachache	☐ Insecure
☐ Rejection	☐ Anxious/Worried
☐ Inability to Concentrate	☐ Achy Joints/Sore Body
☐ Weakness/Lethargy	☐ Guilt
☐ Tension	☐ Unimportant
☐ Depressed	☐ Apathy/Don't Care
☐ Hurt	☐ Change in Appetite
☐ Restlessness	☐ Sleeping Problems
☐ Powerless	☐ Devastation
☐ Guilt	☐ Panic
☐ Tense	☐ Heartache

_____   _____

_____   _____

Pray... *for guidance and peace in your mixed-up thoughts and emotions.*

Helpful Scriptures:

1 Peter 5:7 *Cast all your anxiety on him because he cares for you.*

Matthew 11:28 *(Jesus said) "Come to me, all you who are weary and burdened, and I will give you rest."*

John 14:27 *(Jesus said) "Peace I leave with you; my peace I give you. I do not give you as the world gives. Do not let your hearts be troubled and do not be afraid."*

Psalm 94:19 *When anxiety was great within me, your consolation brought joy to my soul.*

"I am convinced that life is 10% what happens to me and 90% how I react to it. And so it is with you."
—Chuck Swindoll

Grief Stages

You can expect to pass through certain typical stages of grief with no strict order in which they come, and no strict guidelines on how to react.

These are only ideas of stages that you're likely to experience. You may have all or some of these, or you may even go through others. More than likely, you will go back and forth through the stages on your way to recovery.

* The initial reaction to a significant loss is usually **shock**, **disbelief** and **denial**. Recognizing the loss is very important in accepting it.

* There will be a response to the pain and sorrow that varies with each person. There may be a time of **anger** and **mixed-up emotions**. This can be a very hard time, but the hurt should be felt and experienced in full.

* There will be a time of **remembrance**, then a time of **letting go** and **acceptance**. Allow yourself to think about your loved one or what you've lost, remembering everything you can. After a while you will begin to let go of the hurtful things that delay your healing. Acceptance will follow the "letting go" process.

* Eventually you will come to a stage of **rebuilding**. You will be able to redefine who you are, face and actually embrace a "new normal" and a new reality. You will adjust to a new life, gain hope and discover your faith or have a renewal of faith.

There is no "correct way" to move through these stages. You may move forward and then feel a setback. This can happen a lot throughout your journey.

Here is a diagram showing an example of a journey through grief. There are many ups and downs on the graph because you will experience many changes on your journey. You may feel good one day, a high point on the graph, and the next day you could feel like it all crashed down.

Keep on going. Persist forward on your journey no matter how difficult it may seem at times; that is perseverance. If you look at the graph as a whole you will notice it is an overall uphill line—and if you persevere, your journey will look like that, too.

Draw a graph of your own progression. You may want to do this activity occasionally so you can see your own development. Talk to someone about your graph or write about it in your journal.

My grief journey

Pray... *for perseverance through the stages of your grief journey.*

Helpful Scriptures:

James 5:11 *As you know, we consider blessed those who have persevered. You have heard of Job's perseverance and have seen what the Lord finally brought about. The Lord is full of compassion and mercy.*

Psalm 107:6 *Then they cried out to the Lord in their trouble, and he delivered them from their distress.*

Psalm 34:18-19 *The Lord is close to the brokenhearted and saves those who are crushed in spirit.*

2 Corinthians 12:9 *But he said to me, "My grace is sufficient for you, for my power is made perfect in weakness."*

"Grief is a process, not a state."
—Anne Grant

Identify Your Support System

A support system is made up of the **people you trust, who help you and comfort you**. They take care of you and provide emotional support and strength.

Some examples of a support system might include parents, grandparents, siblings, and other family members and relatives. This structure may also include friends, godparents, teachers, coaches, counselors, pastors, doctors, youth group, team members, club members, classmates, and even God.

Identify your support system. Make a list of the people close to you that you can depend on. Are you calling on them when you feel bad or need something? **These people care about you and should be called** upon when you need someone.

Draw a diagram of "Me"
connected to a circle of support with a name at the end of each arrow. (Draw as many arrows as needed.)

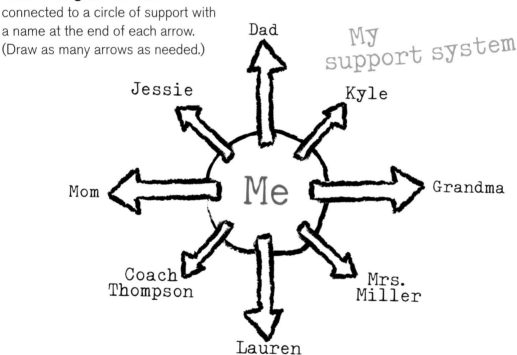

My support system

Dad
Jessie
Kyle
Mom
Me
Grandma
Coach Thompson
Mrs. Miller
Lauren

Pray... *for the people in your support system.*

Helpful Scriptures:

Proverbs 17:17 *A friend loves at all times.*

Luke 22:28 *(Jesus said) You are those who have stood by me in my trials.*

Philippians 1:4 *In all my prayers for all of you, I always pray with joy.*

Psalm 94:18 *When I said, "My foot is slipping," your love, O Lord, supported me.*

"It is amazingly empowering to have the support of a strong, motivated, and inspirational group of people."
–Dr. Susan Jeffers

Allowing the Grief and Pain

With grief there is pain; the two go hand in hand. **Give yourself permission** to explore your feelings that are wrapped up in the pain, and allow the hurt to come.

Pain can be scary, so there is a tendency to hide from it. However, if you don't completely experience the sorrow, it can eventually grow stronger. Be patient and don't rush your grief, but allow it to come.

You will not always feel the way you do right now, so go ahead and enter straight into the grief. You may feel that if you let your guard down to the grief, you will never recover, that you will fall into some dark pit. On the contrary, once you feel the pain, and **give it the time it needs and work through it**, you will see that it begins to diminish and lose its power.

You will notice that pain and grief no longer dominate you, and then slowly, each will begin to subside. As time passes, the pain that once gripped your heart will loosen its hold and you will be able to remember the past with a smile.

By recognizing your loss and agreeing to mourn, you will begin your healing process. Say out loud, *"I allow myself to mourn my loss. I agree to feel the pain on my grief journey because I know I will feel better one day."* Talk with someone in your support system or journal about the way it felt to make that declaration.

Pray... *for strength, comfort and peace as you allow your grief to come.*

Helpful Scriptures:

Psalm 29:11 *The Lord gives strength to his people; the Lord blesses his people with peace.*

John 16:22 *(Jesus said) "Now is your time of grief, but I will see you again and you will rejoice, and no one will take away your joy."*

Matthew 5:4 *(Jesus said) "Blessed are those who mourn, for they will be comforted."*

2 Thessalonians 3:3 *But the Lord is faithful, and he will strengthen and protect you.*

"The best way out is always through."
—Robert Frost

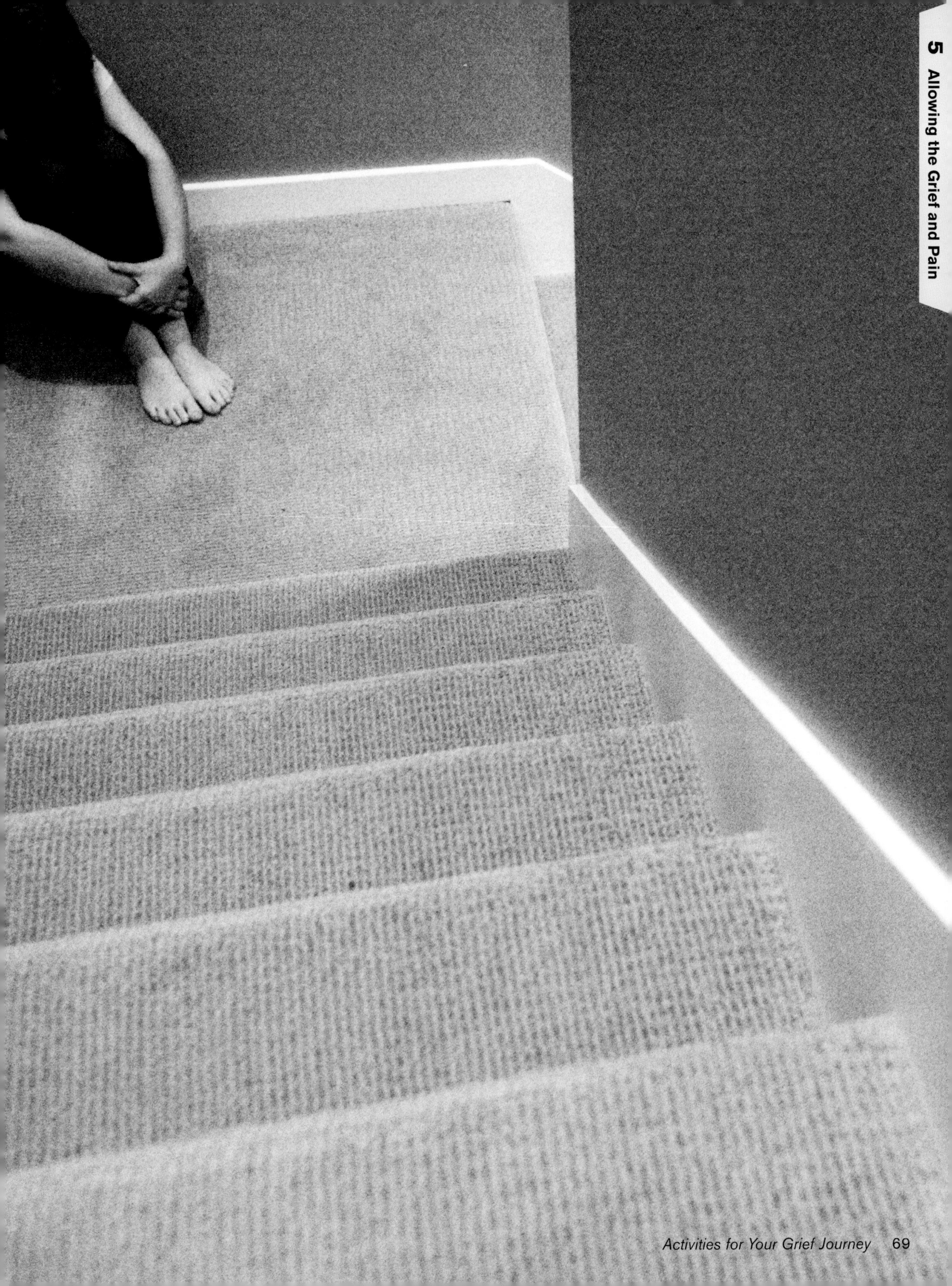

Hole in the Heart

When you lose someone or something you love, you may feel as though a hole is left in your heart.

Even though your heart will never be exactly the same, and your loss can never be replaced, you can still **do things that help fill the empty space that was left**.

What things can you do to help fill the hole in your heart? Use some of these ideas provided, or come up with some of your own. Think about it, and then write the activities down and keep adding ideas until your heart feels better.

After actually participating in some of these activities, you will begin to feel your own heart filling up.

* Show love and affection to your pet, or adopt a pet.

* Give someone a hug.

* Tell someone you love him or her.

* Show kindness and be courteous to others.

* Give someone a compliment.

* Write a letter or send a card to someone who needs it.

* Visit someone who would appreciate it.

* Help others who would benefit from the assistance.

* Meet new friends.

* Have fun with old friends.

* Volunteer your time and effort to someone who deserves it.

* Spend time with the people you love.

* Try a new hobby or craft.

* Play a new game or sport.

* Learn about something interesting.

* Explore your surroundings with someone.

* Tutor another student or teach others something you know.

Pray... *that God will help fill the void in your heart.*

Helpful Scriptures:

2 Thessalonians 2:16-17 *May Jesus himself and God our Father, who reached out in love and surprised you with gifts of unending help and confidence, put a fresh heart in you* (THE MESSAGE).

Psalm 51:10 *Create in me a pure heart, O God, and renew a steadfast spirit within me.*

John 14:1 *(Jesus said) "Do not let your hearts be troubled. Trust in God; trust also in me."*

Isaiah 60:20 *The Lord will be your everlasting light, and your days of sorrow will end.*

"You change your life by changing your heart."
—Max Lucado

Open and Honest

Tell at least one trusted person in your support system how you are doing in your grief journey. Tell them what helps you in your recovery process and what doesn't.

Be truthful when expressing your feelings. Don't just say what you think someone wants to hear. **Talk truthfully about how you feel**, what is going on with you and what you want.

Being open and honest with your thoughts and feelings can release you to move forward in your journey. You could also explain this with detail in your journal if you would like. If you do choose to write it down, take your journal to someone, let him or her read about how you feel, and then discuss it.

Pray... *for an open heart of truth when discussing your feelings.*

Helpful Scriptures:

John 8:32 *(Jesus said) "Then you will know the truth, and the truth shall set you free."*

Psalm 43:3 *Send forth your light and your truth, let them guide me.*

John 16:13 *(Jesus said) "But when he, the Spirit of truth, comes, he will guide you into all truth."*

"Honesty is the first chapter in the book of wisdom."
—Thomas Jefferson

Angry Moments

During the grief journey there may be many times when **anger rises** within you. People can do or say the wrong things that make you angry.

You may feel mad at the person who died, or with someone who caused your loss, or you may even be angry with God.

You could feel mad at the whole world sometimes. There are times you just feel angry! Getting mad occasionally is normal. But if anger stays too long, it can turn into a stronger emotion called rage, and that can turn out of control.

Anger that is not resolved can create bitterness. These are very powerful and negative emotions that you don't want to keep. If you hang onto them for en extended period of time, they can become stumbling blocks in your recovery.

Even though it is typical to feel this way, it is important to get these feelings out. However, **you don't ever want to take your anger out on another person**.

There are some things you can do to release these emotions constructively.

When feeling angry, you can:

* Count to 10 or take several deep breaths.

* Exercise such as jogging or kicking a ball.

* Scribble hard on paper or tear up strips of scrap paper, then wad up the papers and throw it all into the trash; imagine your anger being discarded with the paper.

* Make a drawing of what anger looks like to you.

* Talk to someone in your support system or let it all out in your journal. Explain what makes you angry; be honest and open with your words and don't worry about sounding "right."

* Physically let emotions out. Sometimes expression of anger does not come in words. In those times, you can find a safe place to vent your emotions by yelling, kicking, screaming, stomping your feet, shaking your body, pounding your fists into a pillow, or running as fast as you can. However, if you choose to release your anger in such a way, make sure you **tell someone you trust what you are doing** and always make certain you **remain safe**. You don't ever want to hurt yourself or others while releasing your anger.

You may find that expressing the feelings you have makes you feel better, so let all the anger go from your heart and then replace it with love.

Pray... *for the release of anger in a safe way when it comes.*

Helpful Scriptures:

Ephesians 4:31 Get rid of all bitterness, rage and anger...

Colossians 3:8 But now you must rid yourselves of all such things as these; anger, rage, malice...

Ephesians 4:26 "In your anger do not sin."

Psalm 38:22 Come quickly to help me, O Lord my Savior.

"For every minute you remain angry, you give up sixty seconds of peace of mind."
—Ralph Waldo Emerson

8 Angry Moments

Forgiveness

Forgiveness is essential in your grief journey. Unforgiveness is a destructive emotion and holding onto it may only make your heart feel worse and delay your recovery.

You may need to forgive the person who died, or is no longer in your life. You may need to forgive the person you feel is responsible for your pain. You may need to forgive yourself, or even God.

Maybe you need to forgive the things people have said or done that hurt your feelings or made you mad since your loss. Most people don't intend to be insensitive, so be patient and forgive them.

Whatever the case, forgiveness is huge! It may seem hard or even impossible at first, but it is very important to your progression. If unforgiveness stays too long, it often becomes bitterness and even more. These emotions will eventually make you even sadder and begin to hurt you physically.

Talk to someone in your support system and you can even talk to God about it. He forgave you and He can help you forgive others. Talk about how you feel and whom you need to forgive. You can write a letter to the person you need to forgive but you don't have to send it. Sometimes it just helps to write it. It may also help to write about it in your journal.

Forgiveness comes in time so don't hold back the words that can get the process started. **Let it all out so you can begin to let it all go**.

Pray... *that God help you forgive.*

Helpful Scriptures:

Ephesians 4:32 *Be kind and compassionate to one another, forgiving each other, just as in Christ, God forgave you.*

Matthew 6:14 *(Jesus said) "For if you forgive men when they sin against you, your Father will also forgive you."*

Luke 1:37 *"For nothing is impossible with God."*

Romans 8:37 *In all these things we are more than conquerors through him who loved us.*

"To forgive is the highest, most beautiful form of love. In return, you will receive untold peace and happiness."
—Robert Muller

Pray

Prayer is your time talking to God. You can discuss whatever you wish with Him. There is **no special way to do it**; there are no specific words to say and no particular way to say them. Just call on God in the name of His son Jesus Christ whenever you need Him.

Talk to your Heavenly Father with love and respect and speak to Him as if he were sitting next to you. He is closer than you might think. Tell God openly how you feel and what concerns you. Speak from your heart and your prayers will be heard.

It is good to give thanks for what you have and even pray for others. God loves you and wants you to call on Him.

There is a scripture in the Bible (*1 Thessalonians 5:17*) that says to pray continually. That means you can just talk to God **whenever you like and as often as you wish**. You don't have to be in church to pray; you can talk with God anywhere throughout the day and night. You can talk with him all day long because he never gets tired of hearing from you!

Pray with someone, pray alone or write your prayers to God in your journal. If you are uncomfortable or not sure what to say, read the example of prayer Jesus gave us in the Bible.

> **Matthew 6:9–13** *"This, then, is how you should pray:*
> *Our Father in heaven, hallowed be your name, your kingdom come, your will be done on earth as it is in heaven. Give us today our daily bread. Forgive us our debts, as we also have forgiven our debtors. And lead us not into temptation, but deliver us from the evil one. For yours is the kingdom and the power and the glory forever. Amen."*

Just remember when you pray you are having a **conversation with God**. As with any communication with someone you trust, you want to have an open heart and speak honestly about what is on your mind.

Pray... *for openness, courage, and faith when talking to God.*

Helpful Scriptures:

Philippians 4:6-7 *Do not be anxious about anything, but in everything, by prayer and petition, with thanksgiving, present your requests to God. And the peace of God, which transcends all understanding, will guard your hearts and your minds in Christ Jesus.*

Hebrews 4:16 *Let us then approach the throne of grace with confidence, so that we may receive mercy and find grace to help us in our time of need.*

Ephesians 3:12 *In him and through faith in him we may approach God with freedom and confidence.*

Romans 8:26 *The Spirit helps us in our weakness. We do not know what we ought to pray for, but the Spirit himself intercedes for us with groans that words cannot express.*

"Pray to God, but keep rowing to shore."
—Russian Proverb

Fears Go Away!

Fear can be a normal reaction resulting from tragedy, loss or death of a loved one. You may be afraid of the dark, of being left alone, of being around new people or getting hurt. You may be afraid of death and dying.

You may even develop fears you never had before. You could feel uncertain of what the future holds for you and afraid of what your life will be like.

Fear is just a reaction and **does not have to become a part of who you are**. Identify your fears and talk about them openly or journal them. Don't run from what frightens or worries you. Face your fears head-on; do not hide from them. Deal with them directly and you can drive your fears away.

Pray... *for the release of fear in your life.*

Helpful Scriptures:

Isaiah 43:5 *"Do not be afraid, for I am with you."*

Psalm 34:4 *I sought the Lord, and he answered me; he delivered me from all my fears.*

Psalm 46:1–2 *God is our refuge and strength, an ever-present help in trouble. Therefore we will not fear.*

Hebrews 13:5–6 *God has said, "Never will I leave you; never will I forsake you." So we say with confidence, "The Lord is my helper; I will not be afraid."*

1 John 4:18 *There is no fear in love. But perfect love drives out fear.*

> "No one ever told me that grief felt so like fear."
> —C.S. Lewis

Have you ever said "what-if"…? Do you have any regrets concerning your loss?

The past cannot be changed; however, the "what-ifs" and regrets can be addressed and worked through. **Everyone has done or said things in life to regret**.

Sometimes it is the things not done or not said that cause regret. Whatever the regrets are, it is important to talk about them and then put them behind you. You must identify and work through these issues so your journey through grief can continue.

At some point you must stop looking back with regret and start **focusing on the future**. Talk to someone in your support system about this, or you can journal your concerns. Your progress may be delayed until you deal with and let go of these uncertainties.

Pray... *for the ability to let go of regrets and doubt.*

Helpful Scriptures:

Philippians 3:13 *…forgetting what is behind and straining toward what is ahead.*

Isaiah 43:18-19 *"Forget the former things; do not dwell on the past. See I am doing a new thing!"*

Isaiah 42:9 *See, the former things have taken place, and new things I declare.*

"Holding on to the past and all its mistakes will only hinder you from taking hold of the future that God has planned for you."
—Terri Savelle Foy

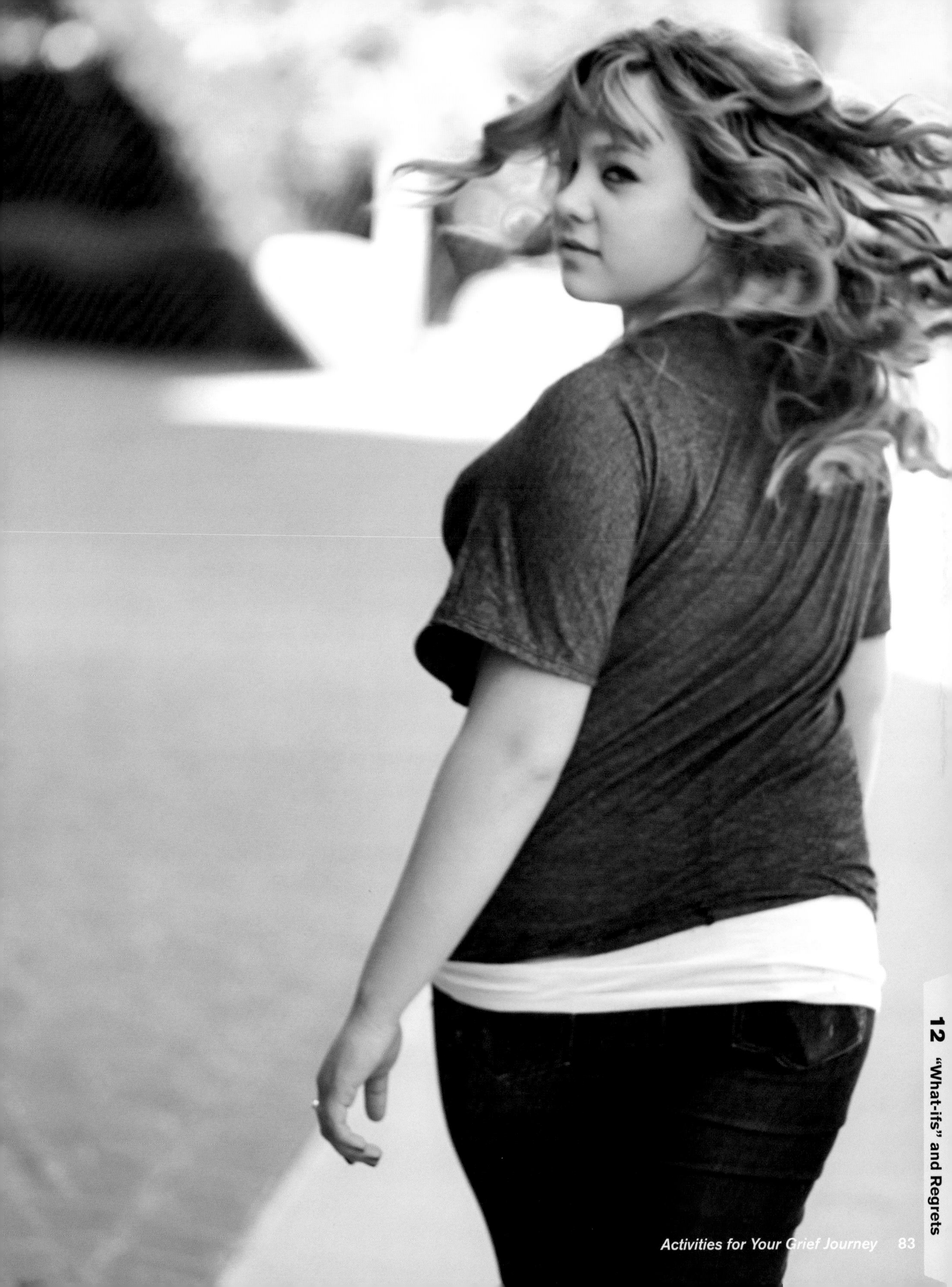

Ask "Why?"

There are so many questions concerning death, loss, or tragedy. Do you find yourself asking "why?" to many different questions? Go ahead, **ask all of the questions that concern you**.

You can ask your questions to a person in your support system or ask God. Write your questions in your journal if you choose. **Know that not all questions will be answered, or even can be answered**. However, you may still receive comfort even without getting all of the answers.

Talking about your doubts and concerns may help ease them, so feel free to communicate and ask. Process and think about the answers you get and concentrate on accepting them. Just be prepared to also accept when there are no answers.

Pray... *for peace and acceptance in the answers revealed and also in the unanswered questions.*

Helpful Scriptures:

Psalm 4:1 *Answer me when I call to you, O my righteous God. Give me relief from my distress; be merciful to me and hear my prayer.*

Isaiah 55:8 *"For my thoughts are not your thoughts, neither are your ways my ways," declares the Lord.*

Psalm 145: 18–19 *The Lord is near to all who call on him, to all who call on him in truth. He fulfills the desires of those who fear him; he hears their cry and saves them.*

"It's OK to ask "why?" Jesus did when He cried out in a loud voice from the cross, "My God, my God, <u>why</u> have you forsaken me?"
—Tim Doyle

"Letting go" does not mean you are to release your love and happy memories of your special person or what you have lost. "Letting go" does not mean you let go of your loved one. You will always have the memories that give you joy.

Your relationships, memories, or that special person will always be a part of you. "Letting go" refers to the **release of the discouraging thoughts and negative emotions that cause pain** and delay progress in recovery. These things can hold you back.

What you let go of is the unforgiveness, fear, "what-ifs," regrets, anger, depression and any other hurtful thoughts and emotions. It is also best to let go of false hopes and expectations.

There will eventually come a time of letting go of the "old world" and readjusting to a new one without your loved one and the familiar things. Just remember that it doesn't mean you let go of the love, joy and happy memories you will always have.

Let go of the things that weigh you down, and **free yourself to progress** further in your recovery. Talk about or journal the things you would like to and need to let go of.

"Some of us think holding on makes us strong but sometimes it is letting go."
—Hermann Hesse

Pray... *for the ability to let go of all negative and destructive thoughts and emotions.*

Helpful Scriptures:

John 8:36 *(Jesus said) "So if the Son sets you free, you will be free indeed."*

Ephesians 3:16 *I pray that out of his glorious riches he may strengthen you with power through his Spirit in your inner being, so that Christ may dwell in your hearts through faith.*

Ephesians 4:23 *...to be made new in the attitude of your minds.*

Psalm 51:12 *Restore to me the joy of your salvation and grant me a willing spirit, to sustain me.*

Take Care of Yourself

It is very important to your recovery that you take care of yourself. Your entire being is made up of three portions:

* **Body**

* **Mind**

* **Spirit**

These cannot be separated. If you keep a good balance of these three important parts of yourself, you will stay healthy and feel so much better.

You must keep your body healthy and strong with good nutrition, daily exercise and plenty of rest.

It is so important to be active and it is best to stay away from too much TV and video games. **Get your body moving; it improves the health of your mind and spirit also**.

Eating disturbances can sometimes occur during grief. There may be a tendency to overeat, under eat, or seek comfort in unhealthy foods. Try to drink more water and eat more fresh fruits and vegetables instead of junk food and sugary snacks.

Sometimes grief can be very exhausting so getting enough rest is very important. Your body, mind and spirit will all benefit from plenty of rest and a good night's sleep.

Remember good hygiene by brushing your teeth and hair, taking regular baths or showers and wearing clean clothes. You feel better when you look your best.

Take care of your mind by reading and learning.

Nurture your spirit through prayer, meditation, and reading your Bible.

Talking to someone in your support system or journaling also helps to relieve stress that can negatively affect the body, mind and spirit.

Grief can be an attack on all three parts of your being, so take care of yourself and **use your energy for your recovery**. Talk to someone about what you can do to take good care of yourself, and list some of those things below.

_____

_____

_____

_____

_____

_____

Pray... *for good health of your body, mind, and spirit.*

Helpful Scriptures:

1 Corinthians 6:20 *...honor God with your body.*

Proverbs 14:30 *A heart at peace gives life to the body...*

1 Corinthians 3:16 *Don't you know that you yourselves are God's temple and that God's Spirit lives in you?*

Isaiah 48:17 *This is what the Lord says—your Redeemer, the Holy One of Israel: "I am the Lord your God, who teaches you what is best for you, who directs you in the way you should go."*

"Take care of your body. It's the only place you have to live."
–Jim Rohn

The Sound of Music

Music can be comforting to the body and soul, especially in a time of pain.

Get in a quiet place to listen to your favorite music. Be still, close your eyes and **completely absorb what you hear**. Don't think of anything with your mind; just feel the music with your heart. Listen to the rhythm, keep the beat, be aware of the melody and become a part of the song.

Put on another style of music you've never listened to, or even try to appreciate the music your loved one enjoyed. Let the sounds of soft music surround you like a warm blanket and comfort you. Next, try a different beat and feel the joy of hard, pounding music as it strengthens you and **replaces the sorrow** in your heart.

Pray... *for the appreciation and joy of music and for the release of emotions through the melody.*

Helpful Scriptures:

Psalm 98:4 *Shout for joy to the Lord, all the earth, burst into jubilant song with music.*

Psalm 13:6 *I will sing to the Lord, for he has been good to me.*

Psalm 147:7 *Sing to the Lord with thanksgiving; make music to our God.*

Psalm 96:1 *Sing to the Lord a new song; sing to the Lord, all the earth.*

Psalm 100:2 *Worship the Lord with gladness; come before him with joyful songs.*

"Music washes away from the soul the dust of everyday life."
—Berthold Auerbach

Remember

Remember and talk about what you have lost. Remember the relationship and the times you spent with your special person and what you miss.

Don't try to forget the good memories because you think it is too painful; **try to remember**. Embrace the memory of what you were blessed with. Imagine talking with the person you have lost; remember the things you talked about. Recall the things she laughed about and remember her smile. Think about what he said or a quirky look he had.

Remember things of your past that you no longer have. **Recollect with joy** and thanksgiving. This may hurt sometimes, but it is good to remember. Sometimes memories fade as time passes; this is okay, too.

Imagine photographs from the past; the older they get, the more they lose their color, and they are not as clear. But those pictures, just like your memories, are still important. Even though they have changed a bit, they are still valuable to you.

Remember your loved one, or what you have lost, by asking questions, sharing stories, looking at photos, listening to tape recordings or watching home movies. Think of ways you can remember what is important. Think about it in your mind, then remember and share with someone or write about your memories in your journal.

Pray... *for recollection of comforting memories and remembrance of happy times.*

Helpful Scriptures:

Philippians 1:3 *I thank my God every time I remember you.*

Ephesians 1:16 *I have not stopped giving thanks for you, remembering you in my prayers.*

Psalm 115:12 *The Lord remembers us and will bless us.*

"The things hardest to bear are sweetest to remember."
—Seneca

Allow yourself the time and the freedom to really cry. Crying is good because it can temporarily release pent up emotional and physical energy.

You may want to cry with someone you trust, or you may choose to cry alone. Cry hard if you need to, and let it all out. Don't suppress your tears; let it flow out until there is no more.

Sometimes you may feel you shouldn't let it all go or you have to be strong and hold it in. It is best to **allow the tears and emotions to flow naturally**. There are times when the tears just come on their own, whenever you least expect it; that is all right.

However, there are times when you can choose to get in a safe place with a trusted person and release all the tears you may have been hold-ing inside. You may feel better, even cleansed inside, from the release of tears and emotion. Afterwards, you may feel exhausted and need to rest or take a nap. Cry when you feel it is necessary, but remember not all people feel the need to cry, and that is okay too. **Let the tears come if they need to**.

> "Tears are the silent language of grief."
> —Voltaire

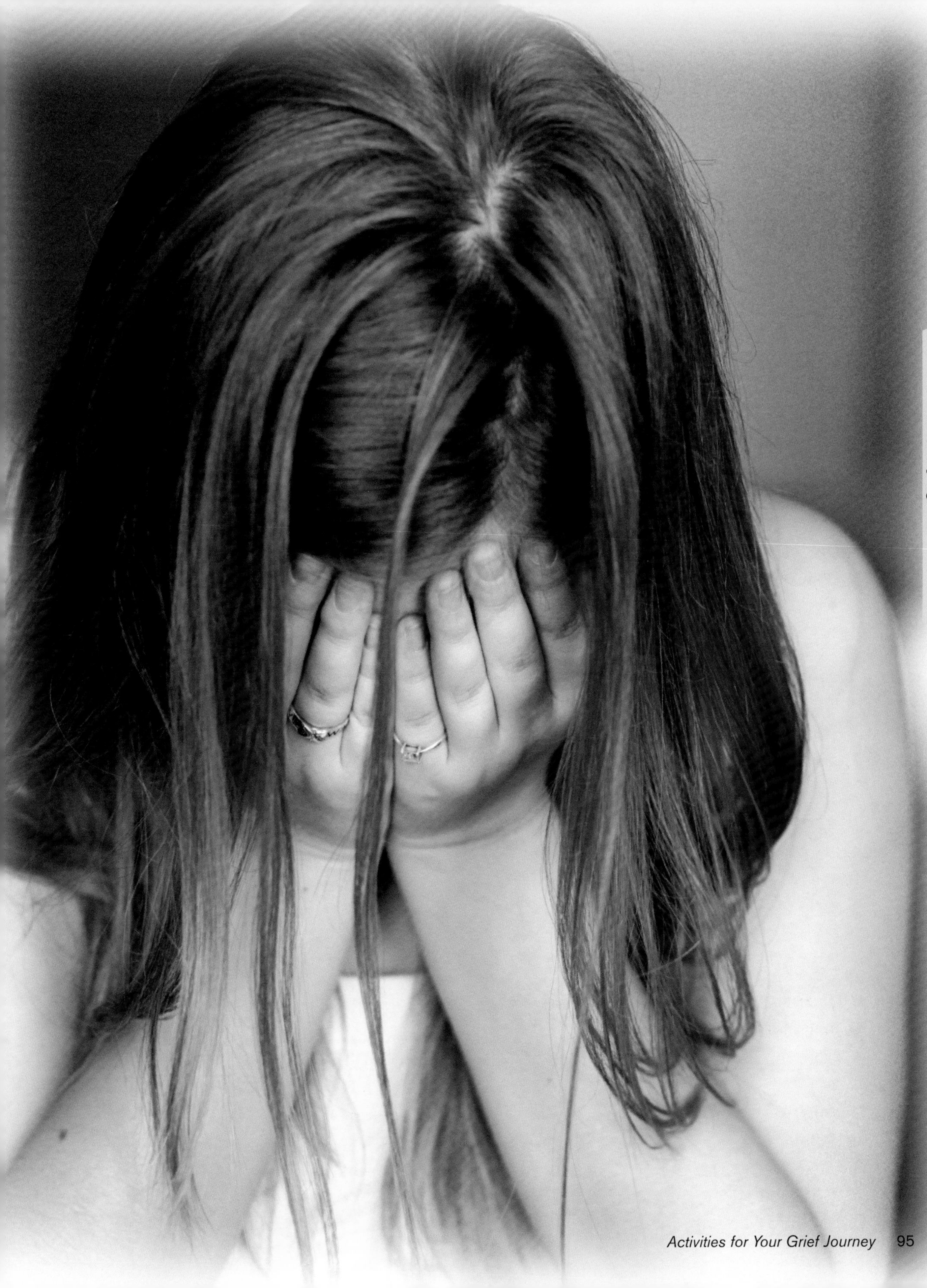

Detours

As with most any trip, there will be delays and detours on your grief journey. Expect them; they are normal. Don't be discouraged by these detours and minor setbacks.

You can recover, **get back on track and continue** on your way to healing. Recovery is your destination, so you will want to keep striving toward that goal, no matter how many detours occur or how often they happen.

What are some of the detours and delays keeping you from your destination? What seems to get in the way of your recovery? Discuss the problems that come up with someone you trust or write about those issues in your journal.

Pray... *for a straight path with no unnecessary detours.*

Helpful Scriptures:

Proverbs 3:5–6 *Trust in the Lord with all your heart and lean not on your own understanding; in all your ways acknowledge him, and he will make your paths straight.*

Proverbs 4:11 *I guide you in the way of wisdom and lead you along straight paths.*

Philippians 3:14 *I press on toward the goal to win the prize for which God has called me heavenward in Christ Jesus.*

"Detours, after all, are temporary."
—Steve Goodier

What is Normal?

You wonder if things will ever get back to normal. It may help you to realize that nothing remains the same throughout life; change is constant. Things change in our lives, even without death or loss.

You may wonder if you will ever feel normal again. Try to remember that "normal" constantly changes throughout our lives, so it is best to embrace and accept that. Don't try to fight it.

Normal as you knew it has changed forever, but that does not mean you cannot be happy with a "new normal". What is normal, anyway? How would you describe what was normal? What do you miss about your "normal" life?

Think about what used to be normal to you and share it with someone or write about it in your journal.

Explore the "new normal" of your life now. How do you see your new life, now and in the future? Express your concerns and hopes for your "new normal". Talk about the negative aspects, but dwell on the positive.

Don't exhaust yourself trying to get your old life back. There are some aspects of your life that may return and some that may not. You cannot put your life back exactly the way it was before, but you can focus on the bright future and the possibilities it holds.

Pray... *for acceptance of your "new normal" with a vision of joy and victory for your future.*

Helpful Scriptures:

1 Peter 5:10 *And the God of all grace, who called you to his eternal glory in Christ, after you have suffered a little while, will himself restore you and make you strong, firm and steadfast.*

Colossians 3:10 *...put on the new self, which is being renewed in knowledge in the image of its Creator.*

Hebrews 13:8 *Jesus Christ is the same yesterday and today and forever.*

"All things must change to something new, to something strange."
—Henry Wadsworth Longfellow

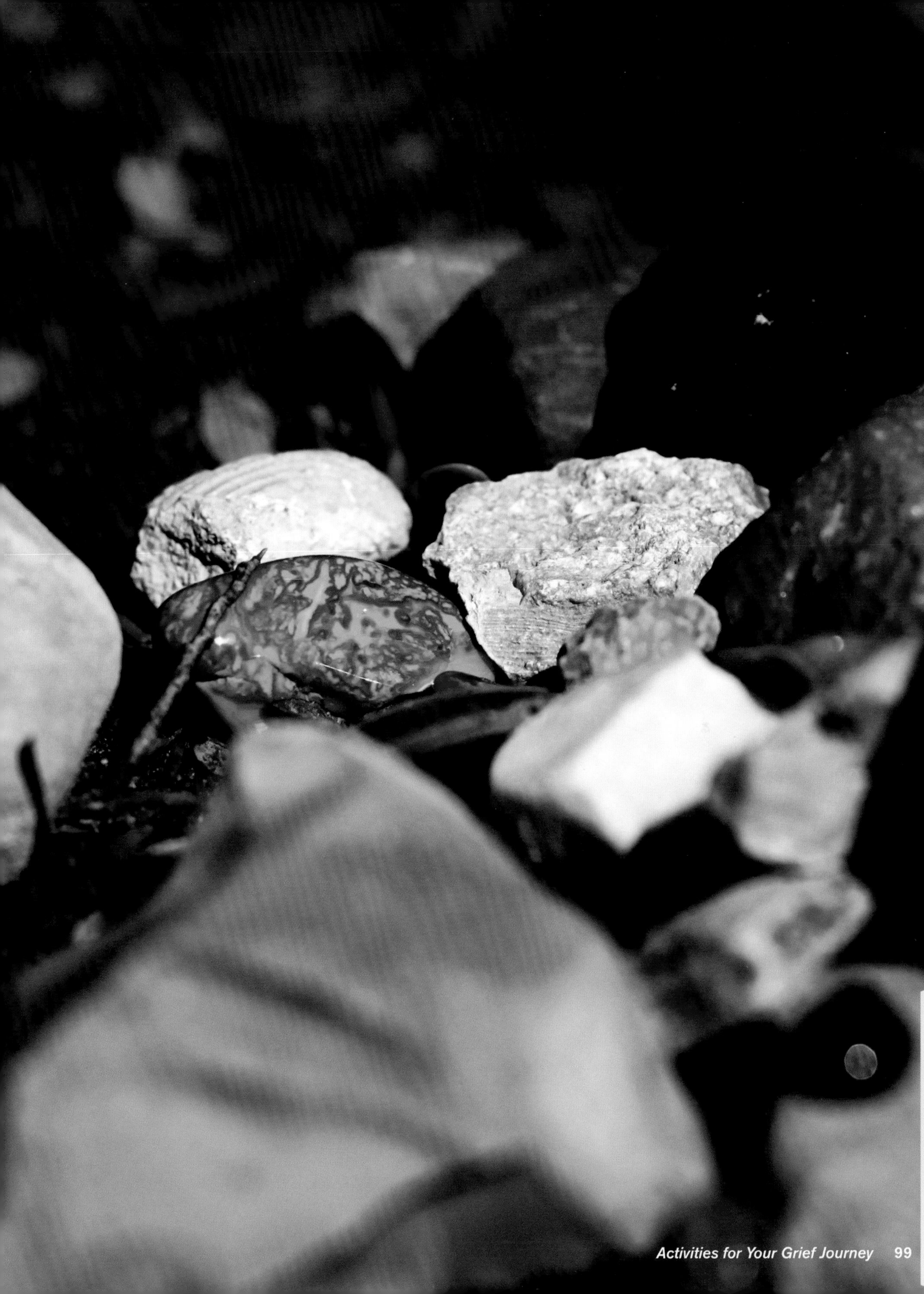

Gratitude List

Feeling grateful makes your heart lighter and more joyful. Think of all the good things in your life that you are grateful for. There are many.

Even your happy memories are to be appreciated. Focus on all the positive around you, and give thanks. You will likely feel more peaceful and content as you concentrate on those good things.

Try to write a list of at least 10 things you are grateful for. Sometimes that may be hard to do when so much is going wrong and you feel so sad. However, if you sit quietly and think hard, you will begin to **find things you are thankful for**. You might begin with basics such as having a place to live, a good school, or plenty of food.

Make a Gratitude List often; try this once a week or at least once a month. It is beneficial to see the good things and the special people in your life written on paper.

My Gratitude List

1.

2.

3.

4.

5.

6.

7.

8.

9.

10.

Pray... *about what is on your Gratitude List and thank God for all of the wonderful blessings in your life.*

> "Gratitude is the heart's memory."
> —French Proverb

Helpful Scriptures:

Psalm 106:1 *Praise the Lord. Give thanks to the Lord, for he is good; his love endures forever.*

1 Thessalonians 5:18 *Give thanks in all circumstances, for this is God's will for you in Christ Jesus.*

Psalm 28:6–7 *Praise be to the Lord, for he has heard my cry for mercy. The Lord is my strength and my shield; my heart trusts in him, and I am helped. My heart leaps for joy and I will give thanks to him in song.*

Power of Positive Thinking

Positive thinking cannot change the past, but it can alter the future. If you think positive thoughts and speak positive words, your life will produce positive results.

You may have painful, confusing times that make you feel hopeless or depressed during your journey through grief. Even though negative thoughts and feelings come, it doesn't mean they have to stay. You can counteract the effects of the negative by dwelling on the positive.

You may feel there is nothing positive in your life to concentrate on, but there is. **Look for the good in your life and the good in yourself**. Speak positive and uplifting words throughout the day.

Be encouraged by scripture and good thoughts. Think of what makes you feel good and uplifted, then try to speak those words to others. When you are running low on positive thoughts, just read some of the statements below and then try to add some of your own.

* **I am valuable** to my family and others.
* **Many people love me.**
* **I am special** and I have a purpose in this life.
* **God loves me** and He will be my strength.
* **I am thankful** for my blessings.
* **I can achieve** great things in my life.
* **I have many gifts** and talents.
* **I can be of service** to someone who needs my help.
* **Good things are in my future.**
* **I will live a happy, victorious life.**

Words of Hope and Encouragement:

Restoration	Healing	Growth
Comfort	Faith	Love
Joy	Happiness	Success
Strength	Perseverance	Powerful
Victory	Overcomer	Determination
Confidence	Assurance	Achievement

Comfort Happy Growth

Joy Strength Success

Victory Overcomer

Faith Healing

Love

Pray... *for the ability to see, appreciate, and dwell on the positive in your life.*

Helpful Scriptures:

Philippians 4:8 ...*Whatever is true, whatever is noble, whatever is right, whatever is pure, whatever is lovely, whatever is admirable—if anything is excellent or praiseworthy—think about such things.*

Proverbs 16:24 *Pleasant words are a honeycomb, sweet to the soul and healing to the bones.*

Deuteronomy 31:8 *The Lord himself goes before you and will be with you; he will never leave you nor forsake you. Do not be afraid; do not be discouraged.*

"Positive thinking will let you do everything better than negative thinking will."
—Zig Ziglar

Be Creative

Be creative in expressing your thoughts and feelings and also in the way you remember your loved one or what you have lost.

Write stories or a poem about your loss and how it makes you feel, or write about the happy memories you have. You could also write about the person you miss.

Create a scrapbook, collage, or a memory album using photos and other mementos of your loved one and your special memories.

Draw, paint, or color pictures depicting the emotions you are experiencing or of the loss you suffered. Maybe you can draw a picture or write a song about or to the loved one you miss.

You could also use crafts to decorate a frame, make jewelry, or build something. You could sculpt with clay, plant a garden, or come up with your own ideas to be creative.

Be free in your expression, it's creative art and it comes from your heart. Use your imagination and create something to release your emotions or to honor your loved one.

Pray... *for your creativity to be revealed in art form.*

Helpful Scriptures:

Deuteronomy 28:12 *The Lord will... bless all the work of your hands.*

Colossians 3:17 *And whatever you do, whether in word or deed, do it all in the name of the Lord Jesus, giving thanks to God the Father through him.*

Philippians 2:13 *For it is God who works in you to will and to act accordingly to his good purpose.*

"Happiness lies in the joy of achievement and the thrill of creative efforts."
—Franklin D. Roosevelt

Sleep Tight

Everyone enjoys a sense of security at night. Regardless of your age, it may feel more "safe and sound" to **cuddle up with something soft** and comforting. It is reassuring to put your arms around an item that can be easily held, and to hug tightly when you need to.

Try sleeping with a favorite stuffed animal, a squishy pillow, or something else soothing. Try sleeping with the comforting object for about a week. Did it help you feel better? Did you feel peaceful or comforted when you went to bed? Tell someone or write in your journal if you think it made a difference in the nighttime. If it does help, continue to "sleep tight" with your special companion for as long as you wish.

Pray... *for a feeling of security.*

Helpful Scriptures:

Psalm 4:8 *I will lie down and sleep in peace, for you alone, O Lord, make me dwell in safety.*

Isaiah 32:18 *My people will live in peaceful dwelling places, in secure homes, in undisturbed places of rest.*

Jeremiah 33:6 *I will heal my people, and will let them enjoy abundant peace and security.*

2 Thessalonians 3:16 *Now may the Lord of peace himself give you peace at all times and in every way. The Lord be with all of you.*

"Good night,
sleep tight,
Wake up bright,
In the morning light,
To do what is right
With all your might."
—Nursery Rhyme

The Cookie Jar

Helplessness is a terrible feeling when you are grieving. At times, your emotions may be out of control when you feel there is nothing you can do to change the situation.

Sometimes a **structured activity** is just what you need to get you out of a dark place and moving into a more constructive and peaceful direction. Instead of reaching into a cookie jar for a sweet treat, reach into "The Cookie Jar" for an activity to do when you are feeling sad, hurt, angry, or confused.

It is helpful to release negative energy in a positive way. Here are some ideas you can use; just write them on a slip of paper and put them in your cookie jar. Think of some other activities you can do that will make you feel better, write them down and put them in your jar also. **Reach into "The Cookie Jar"** whenever you feel overwhelmed or need to refocus your energy, and then do the activity suggested.

If you prefer, you could create a **virtual "Cookie Jar"** using the same activities. Tape the pieces of paper on a mirror, in your locker, or another place you will see them when you need ideas to get you going.

* **READ** your favorite book, a new book, magazine, or the Bible.

* Take a **WALK**.

* **RIDE** your bike or take a **DRIVE**.

* **LAUGH** — Have a contest of making funny faces with your family, a friend, or by yourself in the mirror.

* **BAKE** cookies to give away or try a new recipe to **COOK**.

* **EXERCISE** — Do jumping jacks, swim, walk, jog in place or go running.

* **LOVE A PET** — Talk to your fish, hug your dog, play with your cat or cuddle your lizard.

* **DANCE** — Turn on your favorite music and dance away.

* **TALK** — Call a friend, sit and talk with a loved one, or you can even talk to your pet.

* **GO OUTSIDE** — Enjoy the sunshine, play in the water sprinkler, smell the flowers, pull weeds, breathe in fresh air.

* **GO TO A PARK** or **PLAYGROUND** — Play on as many rides as you can. Swinging can be especially fun.

* **LISTEN TO MUSIC** or **SING**.

* Enjoy any form of **ART**.

Pray... *for the will to do something constructive, to take positive action.*

Helpful Scriptures:

1 Peter 1:13 *Therefore, prepare your minds for action; be self-controlled; set your hope fully on the grace to be given to you when Jesus Christ is revealed.*

Isaiah 41:13 *For I am the Lord, your God, who takes hold of your right hand and says to you, Do not fear; for I will help you.*

2 Corinthians 9:8 *And God is able to make all grace abound to you, so that in all things at all times, having all that you need, you will abound in every good work.*

"Every time you acquire a new interest, even more, a new accomplishment, you increase your power of life."
—William Lyon Phelps

Giving and Receiving

Recall the things your loved one gave you. Maybe you received something tangible like a unique birthday present, a prized trinket or a photo of you two together.

However, you may also remember the things he or she gave you that cannot be held in your hand, like your blue eyes, a sense of humor, piggyback rides, or happy memories.

Did your loved one teach you something that you will never forget? Did he or she tell you stories, show you a skill or craft, or teach you a song? Write down in your journal or talk to someone about all the different things you can think of that your loved one gave to you.

Then **think of all the things that you gave your loved one**. Did you give a special gift, draw a picture or make something at school especially for him or her? Did you give big hugs, kisses or lots of love? Make a list of the things you gave to your special person.

Write down or talk to someone about everything you remember concerning giving and receiving.

Pray... *with a thankful heart for the gifts you have received and for the gifts you have given.*

Helpful Scriptures:

2 Corinthians 9:15 *Thanks be to God for his indescribable gift!*

Acts 10:31 *"God has heard your prayer and remembered your gifts."*

Matthew 7:11 *How much more will your Father in heaven give good gifts to those who ask him!*

"As I give, I get."
—Mary McLeod Bethune

Treasure Chest

Create a box of a few things that represent and remind you of the person who was special to you. These items may be your own things, articles that belonged to your loved one or things you choose in memory of him or her.

You may have something that your loved one gave to you, or you may have something that the two of you shared. These things are valuable to you.

You may choose one or many different items to put in a jewelry box or special container. You could even decorate a shoebox as your own special treasure chest to hold the cherished items.

The choices for your chest could be items that belong to you or your loved one, old or new stuff; it could be anything or lots of things! If you want, you could show the prized possessions in your treasure chest to your family and friends and share with them the stories of the things you have collected and why they are important. They may even have something to share with you that could be added to your collection.

You could also journal about the pieces in your treasure chest and their significance. Enjoy the objects that link you to someone special and allow those items to remind you of your loved one with joy and pleasant memories. Your treasure chest can be a **connection to your loved one** that will carry on.

Ideas for your Treasure Chest:

Photograph	Seashell from the beach	ID card
Ticket stub	Fishing tackle	Watch
Jewelry	Baseball cap	Birthday card
Unusual rock	Golf tee	Old keys

Pray... *with thanksgiving that you have things that remind you of happy times.*

Helpful Scriptures:

Philemon 1:7 *Your love has given me great joy and encouragement, because you, brother, have refreshed the hearts of the saints.*

Psalm 118:29 *Give thanks to the Lord, for he is good; his love endures forever.*

Isaiah 26:3–4 *You will keep in perfect peace him whose mind is steadfast, because he trusts in you. Trust in the Lord forever, for the Lord, the Lord, is the Rock eternal.*

> "To live in the hearts we leave behind is not to die."
> —Thomas Campbell

Space Invaders

It can be comforting for grievers to spend some time **in their loved ones' spaces**. It can be helpful to explore what their interests were and the things that gave them joy. It may be comforting to eat at their favorite restaurant, try their favorite food, sing their favorite song, play their favorite game, cozy up in their favorite chair, participate in their favorite sport or visit a favorite spot. Think about where your loved one liked to spend his or her time and then explore the things he or she liked to do.

It could be challenging yet rewarding to try putting yourself in his or her place and find out why these things and places were enjoyed so much. Whether you're separated from your loved one because of distance or death, this activity may help you feel closer to the person you miss. It can also be a way for the legacy of your loved one to live on in your life.

Remember and talk about the **things concerning your loved one** and the things he or she said, did, and liked. Did you enjoy some of the same things? Did you both enjoy old western movies, playful puppies, hamburgers with no pickles, practical jokes, fishing or star gazing?

Explore thoroughly and find out all you can, then "invade the space" of your loved one. After your discoveries, experience those things for yourself.

This activity may take some time. You may choose to look into one or two things or you may choose to dig into several different areas. Whatever the case, take your time and enjoy the process of discovery.

After you have investigated and participated as a "space invader," reflect on what you found out. Was it comforting to experience the things your special person was interested in? Did it help you in any way? Feel free to talk about or journal your experiences.

Pray... *for a positive connection and comforting feelings while exploring new things.*

Helpful Scriptures:

Isaiah 66:13 *"As a mother comforts her child, so will I comfort you."*

Isaiah 49:13 *For the Lord comforts his people and will have compassion on his afflicted ones.*

Psalm 116:5–6 *The Lord is gracious and righteous; our God is full of compassion. The Lord protects the simplehearted; when I was in great need, he saved me.*

"The pain passes, but the beauty remains."
—Pierre-Auguste Renoir

Sweet Dreams or Nightmares?

Sometimes as you sleep you may have sweet dreams, frightening dreams, or nightmares. You may dream at night about your loved one who died, or about your loss.

Some of these dreams may be **disturbing** to you. However, sometimes you may have **positive and happy** dreams. Try to remember what you can when you wake up so you can deal with what is on your mind and heart. Many fears, hopes, and concerns come out in a person's dreams, so it is very important to talk about your dreams or journal about them.

You will feel better to release your worries rather than cover them up, and it is always nice to share your pleasant dreams with others. Talk about your dreams with someone and discuss how they made you feel.

Pray... *for peaceful dreams and restful sleep.*

Helpful Scriptures:

Proverbs 3:24 *When you lie down, you will not be afraid; when you lie down, your sleep will be sweet.*

Exodus 33:14 *The Lord replied, "My presence will go with you, and I will give you rest."*

Psalm 30:5 *...weeping may remain for a night, but rejoicing comes in the morning.*

Psalm 27:5 *For in the day of trouble he will keep me safe in his dwelling.*

"The best bridge between despair and hope is a good night's sleep."
—E. Joseph Cossman

Living Memorial

There is something comforting, even healing, in the presence of nature. Plant a living memorial in remembrance of your loved one so you can enjoy its beauty while honoring someone special.

You may choose to plant a tree, a shrub, herbs, or flowers. Nurturing a living thing and watching it grow strong and beautiful over time can be **helpful to your recovery**.

As your living memorial grows and develops, you will see that you do, too. Just like the plant you choose, you will become stronger and more resilient with time and care.

There are **many ways to honor** your loved ones or what you've lost, and **keep those positive memories alive**. Look at the list below or come up with some of your own ideas, then talk to someone about how you would like to participate in a "living memorial."

Ways to honor and memorialize:

* Plant in a garden, public park, or near the place of death. (Get permission when necessary.)
* Keep a potted plant or flower; either your loved one's favorite, a type you enjoy, or one from the funeral.
* Create a scholarship fund.
* Create a foundation in your loved one's name.
* Donate to a favorite charity.
* Write a memorial article for the local newspaper.
* Participate in charity events or walk/run in honor or in memoriam.
* Place a memorial plaque somewhere special.
* Launch a balloon with a note or message inside.
* "Adopt" a threatened or endangered animal.
* Have a star named after your loved one.
* Create an online memorial.
* Volunteer your time to a special group or organization.

Pray... *for receiving comfort in what you plant or sow.*

Helpful Scriptures:

Psalm 126:5 *Those who sow in tears will reap with songs of joy.*

Revelation 22:2 *And the leaves of the tree are for the healing...*

James 3:18 *Peacemakers who sow in peace raise a harvest of righteousness.*

"Praising what is lost makes the remembrance dear."
—William Shakespeare

Stay Active

During this time, it helps to keep your body and mind active. You want to avoid doing nothing, which can lead to isolation or depression.

However, you want to **stay busy without overdoing it**. Be careful not to overload yourself with activities to the point of exhaustion or avoidance of the grief process. It is important to keep your mind and body active, but not on a schedule that is overwhelming or adds to the stress in your life. There is a healthy balance of activity and rest in your life, and it may take a little time to find it.

There are **many activities to keep you moving** in a healthy direction. You could ride a bike, take walks, exercise, take classes, join clubs, read books, dance, play your favorite sport, volunteer, or take your dog for a walk. Think of activities you would enjoy, talk to others for even more suggestions, and then try different ways to stay active.

Pray... *for the strength to stay active.*

Helpful Scriptures:

Isaiah 40:29–31 *He gives strength to the weary and increases the power of the weak. Even youths grow tired and weary, and young men stumble and fall; but those who hope in the Lord will renew their strength. They will soar on wings like eagles; they will run and not grow weary, they will walk and not be faint.*

Isaiah 40:31 *...those who hope in the Lord will renew their strength.*

Psalm 121:8 *The Lord will watch over your coming and going both now and forevermore.*

2 Timothy 1:7 *For God did not give us a spirit of timidity, but a spirit of power, of love and of self-discipline.*

"The only cure for grief is action."
–G.H. Lewes

Holidays and Special Days

Birthdays, holidays, anniversaries and other special days can be particularly difficult after a death or loss. This is a very important time for families to talk and communicate with each other.

People deal with loss differently and may have **diversified views on how to approach these special days**. All family members' expectations should be considered during these times. What is comfortable and desired by each person may vary, so to avoid confusion, **discuss openly as a family unit**.

Let your desires and ideas be known to your family and support system. Here are a few suggestions for remembering and **honoring your loved one**, or what you lost, on very special days. However, you and your family can come up with your own ideas. It doesn't matter what you do to recognize your loss or how you celebrate these days, as long as you feel comfortable doing it.

* Make a card or buy a card for your loved one.

* Draw a picture of a special memory concerning the special day.

* Share stories and memories of the special days you celebrated in the past.

* As a family, participate in a special activity together and have fun while remembering.

* Light a candle or set a place at the table in memory of a loved one during a special mealtime.

* Watch home movies of previous holidays and special days.

* Make a special ornament using a photo of your loved one or of a family memory.

* Look through photos and scrapbooks together as a family.

* Make new traditions with family and friends concerning a special day or holiday.

Pray... *with thanksgiving for the joyful memories of celebration and for the many happy celebrations to come.*

Helpful Scriptures:

Proverbs 10:7 *The memory of the righteous will be a blessing.*

Psalm 145:7 *They will celebrate your abundant goodness and joyfully sing of your righteousness.*

1 Corinthians 14:33 *For God is not a God of disorder but of peace.*

Proverbs 15:13 *A happy heart makes the face cheerful, but heartache crushes the spirit.*

1 Chronicles 16:27 *Splendor and majesty are before him; strength and joy in his dwelling place.*

> "May you look back on the past with as much pleasure as you look forward to the future."
> —Paul Dickson

Our family picnic

Christmas, 1996

Acceptance

Acceptance of your loss and of your new life is **vital to the progression** in your grief journey. Accepting your "new normal" is not forgetting your loved one or your past; it is just moving forward into your future and a healthy recovery.

It is important to accept the loss and the changes it has created in your life. Desperately trying to return your life to the way it was before is not only frustrating, but it can also be exhausting. Your life as you knew it has changed forever; things will not be the same again. Even though things have changed, that doesn't mean you can't have a happy and rewarding life.

There is **hope for your future**, a wonderful and fulfilled future. To accept the "new normal" of your present life and what is to come, you must first identify what you think that is.

Make a list of all things that have changed, or will change, in your life since your loss. Make a list of things that have not changed. Now, create a list for your new life; write on paper what you see the future as. Try to be as positive as possible while creating your list. Come back and do this activity again later in your recovery and compare to see how your list has changed over time. Share your lists and concerns with someone in your support system or write about it in your journal.

Change	No Change	New Life

Pray... *for acceptance of your loss and of your new life.*

Helpful Scriptures:

Jeremiah 29:11 *"For I know the plans I have for you," declares the Lord, "plans to prosper you and not to harm you, plans to give you hope and a future."*

Isaiah 41:10 *So do not fear, for I am with you; do not be dismayed, for I am your God. I will strengthen you and help you; I will uphold you with my righteous right hand.*

Psalm 30:2 *O Lord my God, I called to you for help and you healed me.*

Revelation 21:5 *He who was seated on the throne said, "I am making everything new!"*

"God, grant me the serenity to accept the things I cannot change, courage to change the things I can, and wisdom to know the difference."
—Serenity Prayer

Saying Good-bye

In some cases, death comes unexpectedly before you have a chance to say good-bye.
Maybe you knew that death was coming, but you were unable to talk with your loved one.

You may feel angry about not being able to talk to him or her one last time. **You may feel cheated out of your "good-bye,"** because you didn't get to say everything you wanted to say.

Now is the time for you to say good-bye to your loved one. Write a letter, write in your journal, or say out loud what is on your heart. What would you say if you were now able to say your good-bye?

You may choose to do this alone or

have someone you trust with you. This is your chance to verbalize all your thoughts and feelings to your loved one and officially tell him or her good-bye. This does not mean that you can never "talk" with that person again; this is just saying good-bye.

Pray... *for the ability to release and say "good-bye" with peace.*

Helpful Scriptures:

2 Corinthians 13:11 *Finally, brothers, good-by...live in peace. And the God of love and peace will be with you.*

Psalm 138:3 *When I called, you answered me; you made me bold and stouthearted.*

Revelation 21:4 *He will wipe every tear from their eyes.*

"Every goodbye is the birth of a memory."
—Dutch Proverb

Writing Your Own Obituary

An obituary is a short account of a person's life after his or her death. You may have seen your loved one's or someone else's obituary written in the newspaper.

In this activity, you are asked to write your own obituary. This exercise may seem a bit strange, or even too difficult, since you are still alive! However, many people, in all kinds of circumstances, have used this exercise to make them more aware of what they expect from themselves and where they want their lives to go. It is never too early to have direction for your life with positive hopes and dreams.

Even the youngest of grievers can tell what they want people to say about them, what they would like to be when they grow up and what they would like to do later in life. Everyone has dreams. Stretch yourself, even out of your comfort zone, to participate in this activity. **Search your inner thoughts and feelings to see what you can come up with**.

Some of the younger participants may need help with this, but the results will be worth the effort. Write your "obituary" as you would like it to be someday after you have lived your life to the fullest. It is interesting to see the characteristics you desire, what you want to do with your life, and what you would like people to say about you when you're gone. Once you have written your "obituary," you may be **more aware of who you are and what you want to become**. After you have finished this activity, you can journal or talk about what you discovered.

Pray... *for the ability to see yourself in a strong, positive way to accomplish big dreams and reach huge goals in your life.*

Helpful Scriptures:

Psalm 138:8 *The Lord will fulfill his purpose for me.*

2 Thessalonians 2:16–17 *May our Lord Jesus Christ himself and God our Father, who loved us and by his grace gave us eternal encouragement and good hope, encourage your hearts and strengthen you in every good deed and word.*

Philippians 1:6 *Being confident of this, that he who began a good work in you will carry it on to completion until the day of Christ Jesus.*

Psalm 57:2 *I cry out to God Most High, to God, who fulfills his purpose for me.*

Psalm 16:11 *You have made known to me the path of life; you will fill me with joy in your presence.*

"You have to know what you want to get it."
—Gertrude Stein

After the last activity of writing your own obituary, **you may have created some goals for your future without even realizing it**. What are the things you want to do in the future? What are some of your dreams and aspirations?

They could be small goals like finishing reading the new book someone gave you or making the track team, or you could set a more challenging goal like becoming a doctor or firefighter!

Don't hold back on your goals because they don't sound realistic or logical. These are your dreams and goals; it is not a "to-do" list.

Since they are yours and yours alone, set your goals high and make your dreams big! Make a list of all the things you would like to accomplish now and in the years ahead. Talk about or journal your new goals and desires. Just remember, your dreams and ambitions can never be too large and they are never silly. Your desired achievements are very important.

Pray... *for the ability to set outstanding new goals for your future.*

Helpful Scriptures:

Philippians 4:13 *I can do everything through him who gives me strength.*

Psalm 20:4 *May he give you the desire of your heart and make all your plans succeed.*

Proverbs 16:3 *Commit to the Lord whatever you do, and your plans will succeed.*

Proverbs 16:9 *In his heart a man plans his course, but the Lord determines his steps.*

Psalm 138:8 *The Lord will fulfill his purpose for me; your love, O Lord, endures forever.*

"You can be anything you want to be, have anything you desire, accomplish anything you set out to accomplish... if you will hold to that desire with singleness of purpose."
—Robert Collier

Dance Like No One is Watching

Dancing is an activity of rhythmic body movements, and it can also be a wonderful release of emotions. Dance freely to the music of your choice and **use your body to express how you feel**.

Dance without restraint; use flowing movements that blend into the music, or dance wildly, expressing every emotion you have stored up. One by one, release all of your feelings with your body's actions. The key to releasing yourself to dance is freedom. Shut your bedroom door and let it out. Feel free to express yourself and let out any emotions you may have bottled up inside. Don't worry about anyone seeing you, and don't be concerned about making the "correct" moves.

Dance slowly with your eyes closed or dance like crazy! Just **let it all go to the music**. This is your dance; you can make up your own moves and dance any way you want to. Enjoy yourself and dance like no one is watching.

Pray... *for the freedom to dance.*

Helpful Scriptures:

Ecclesiastes 3:1, 4 *There is a time for everything, and a season for every activity under heaven: a time to mourn and a time to dance.*

Psalm 30:11 *You (The Lord) turned my wailing into dancing.*

Psalm 149:3 *Let them praise his name with dancing.*

Psalm 118:14 *The Lord is my strength and my song; he has become my salvation.*

"To dance is to be out of yourself. Larger, more beautiful, more powerful."
—Agnes de Mille

Helping Another Griever

You know how it feels to grieve, so you may be able to relate and **comfort someone else who is hurting**.

Do you know someone else who has experienced a loss? You don't need to worry about saying the right thing or offering good advice. Just letting someone know that you are a griever, too, and that you care, could make him or her feel better and less isolated.

Let another griever know that you are interested and that you care. Listen carefully and let the griever share openly. Don't try to take away the pain, "fix" the situation, or offer too many suggestions. Just share the moment with him or her. Your presence alone can be encouraging and comforting. Try to be patient and allow silence. It doesn't have to be awkward when no one is speaking, sometimes it is necessary. Words aren't always needed and just a hug or smile can help ease another's pain.

Find ways you could be of practical help to the griever. Does she need help cleaning her room? Can you walk his dog? Ask how you could help.

You could also be a valuable asset to a grief support group. Ask someone in your support system if they have suggestions of ways for you to help if you choose to. It may even help you feel better to **share with other grievers** while offering them support and love.

Pray... *that you can be a help to others who are grieving.*

Helpful Scriptures:

Romans 12:15 *Rejoice with those who rejoice; mourn with those who mourn.*

John 15:12 *(Jesus said) "My command is this: Love each other as I have loved you."*

Proverbs 15:30 *A cheerful look brings joy to the heart, and good news gives health to the bones.*

2 Corinthians 1:3–4 *Praise be to the God and Father of our Lord Jesus Christ, the Father of compassion and the God of all comfort, who comforts us in all our trouble, so that we can comfort those in any trouble with the comfort we ourselves have received from God.*

"After the verb 'to Love,' 'to Help' is the most beautiful verb in the world."
—Bertha von Suttner

Smile

When you are grieving, it may seem impossible to smile. How can you smile after a tragedy? How can you smile when it hurts so badly inside? In these times, joy may seem out of reach.

However, in the fleeting times you remember something happy, or when someone says something funny… know that **it is okay to feel joy**; it is okay to smile.

Smiling is a good thing; it seems to make you feel better by relieving the tension and sadness. Just because you feel the freedom to smile doesn't mean you aren't hurting. The pain may still be present, and you may even feel sad when a smile comes.

Sometimes the joy and sadness are all mixed together, and that is normal.

Feel the freedom of expressing both sorrow and joy. Happiness is a blessing, a gift to be treasured and shared. Even in the middle of your sorrow, you can still **be happy and feel the joy of life**; you can still smile when you want to.

Pray... *for joy and the ability to smile.*

Helpful Scriptures:

John 16:20 *You will grieve, but your grief will turn to joy.*

Philippians 4:4 *Rejoice in the Lord always. I will say it again: Rejoice!*

1 Thessalonians 5:16 *Be joyful always.*

Isaiah 55:12 *You will go out in joy and be led forth in peace.*

"Every time you smile at someone, it is an action of love, a gift to that person, a beautiful thing."
—Mother Teresa

Have Fun!

Yes, have fun. It is so important to have joy in life, even during painful times. It's okay to have fun and express enjoyment, especially during the sorrow.

Let go of the grief for a moment and allow your heart to be light. **It is not a betrayal to have fun**. You are not being disloyal to your loved one who is no longer with you or to anyone else.

You do not need permission to enjoy life; it is what you should do. You also need to **laugh, and laugh hard**. It may be difficult at first, and it may seem even awkward, but think of ways you could try to enjoy yourself. Ask friends or family members for ideas. Maybe you could play a game like "freeze-tag" or "hide and seek," no matter what your age. There is something therapeutic about the physical action and just being in the moment of the game.

* Try taking photos while making silly faces or jumping.

* You could also watch cartoons, a funny movie or a comedy on TV.

* Skip outside, let go and allow the joy to come.

* Have a contest with someone to see who can laugh the hardest. Laughter is contagious and healthful to your body and soul; so **permit yourself to have fun** and laugh.

Talk openly about your feelings on having fun. Do you feel you are ready to do fun things again? Do you have any reservations or concerns about enjoying yourself? Does it feel odd, or do you miss it? Discuss your feelings with someone in your support system. After you have engaged in playful activities, you may want to share your experiences in your journal or with someone. Explain what was effective and also what it felt like to laugh and have fun again.

Pray... *for the ability to laugh and have fun without guilt.*

Helpful Scriptures:

Ecclesiastes 3:1, 4 *There is a time for everything, and a season for every activity under heaven: a time to weep and a time to laugh, a time to mourn and a time to dance.*

Luke 6:21 *(Jesus said) "Blessed are you who weep now, for you will laugh."*

Job 8:21 *He will yet fill your mouth with laughter and your lips with shouts of joy.*

Jeremiah 31:13 *I will turn their mourning into gladness; I will give them comfort and joy instead of sorrow.*

Isaiah 51:11 *Gladness and joy will overtake them, and sorrow and sighing will flee away.*

"Fun is good."
—Dr. Seuss

Activities for Your Grief Journey 139

Resources

The following are a few resources for young people needing help. This is not a comprehensive list and does not substitute for a counselor, doctor or professional therapy when necessary.

Boys Town National Hotline
Boys and girls
24 hours, all ages, all concerns
800-448-3000
www.boystown.org
Boys Town assistance for teens:
www.yourlifeyourvoice.org

Youth America Hotline!
Any crisis, 24 hours
877-YOUTHLINE (877-968-8454)
www.youthline.us

National Suicide Prevention Lifeline
With Help Comes Hope
1-800-273-TALK (8255)
www.suicidepreventionlifeline.org

Online resources

www.griefrecoverykit.com

www.helpguide.org

www.grief.com

www.journeyofhearts.org

www.grieflossrecovery.com

www.journeyanswers.com

www.grief.net

www.griefshare.org

My Journal

_____

_____

_____

_____

_____

_____

_____

_____

_____

_____

_____

_____

_____

"The most beautiful people we have known are those who have known defeat, known suffering, known struggle, known loss, and have found their way out of the depths. These persons have an appreciation, a sensitivity and an understanding of life that fills them with compassions, gentleness, and a deep loving concern. Beautiful people do not just happen." **—Elisabeth Kübler-Ross**